Luella is a gifted storyteller! As a secondary school educator myself, I could relate to some of the situations she experienced and the personalities she encountered. I could "hear" the characters in my head as I read the book and found myself nodding or shaking my head when I wasn't laughing. If you enjoy watching *Abbott Elementary*, then you'll love reading this book.
> — Sergio Diaz, World Languages Instructor, St. Francis High School, La Cañada, CA, and Voiceover for *Bloom Where You Are Planted*

A must-read that will inspire you to do what you were created to do. A book to have on your shelf for a re-read when you need the inspiration. Full of colors! Full of life! Thank you, Luella!
> — Michelle Claire Pentreath, Actress, *Guys and Dolls* performed at Los Angeles Pierce College and Our Lady of Lourdes Church, Northridge

Luella's time on the reservation gave her an appreciation of Native American ways and traditions that shines through in her play and in her memoir.
> — Joe Vasquez, Blackfoot Nation, Voiceover for *Bloom Where You Are Planted*.

Teacher in the Yellow House

My Year on a Montana Reservation

First Edition

© 2024 Luella Wagner, All Rights Reserved

Snow Crocus Publishing
www.snowcrocuspublishing.com

Woodland Hills, California

Publisher's Cataloging-in-Publication data

Names: Wagner, Luella, author.

Title: Teacher in the yellow house : my year on a Montana reservation / Luella Wagner.

Description: Includes bibliographical references. | Woodland Hills, CA: Snow Crocus Publishing, 2024.

Identifiers: LCCN: 2024905886 | ISBN: 978-1-7364209-5-9 (hardcover) | 978-1-7364209-4-2 (paperback) | 978-1-7364209-7-3 (ebook) | 978-1-7364209-6-6 (audio)
Subjects: LCSH Wagner, Luella. | Teachers—Biography. | High school teachers—Montana—Northern Cheyenne Indian Reservation—Biography. | Indian high school students—Montana—Northern Cheyenne Indian Reservation—Biography. | Teacher-student relationships—Montana—Northern Cheyenne Indian Reservation. | Northern Cheyenne Indian Reservation (Mont.)—Biography—Anecdotes. | Catholic Church—Education—United States. | BISAC BIOGRAPHY & AUTOBIOGRAPHY / Memoirs | BIOGRAPHY & AUTOBIOGRAPHY / Educators
Classification: LCC LB885 .W34 2024 | DDC 370/.1—dc23

Cover design: Caroline Green

Editor: Adele Field

Scripture taken from the HOLY BIBLE, NEW INTERNATIONAL VERSION. COPYRIGHT © 1973, 1978, 1984 International Bible Society. Used by permission of Zondervan Bible Publishers

Without limiting the rights under copyright reserved above, no part of this publication may be reproduced, stored in or introduced into a retrieval system, or transmitted in any form or by any means (electronic, mechanical, photocopying, recording, or otherwise), without the prior written permission of both the copyright owner and the above publisher of this book, except by a reviewer who wishes to quote brief passages in connection with a review written for insertion in a magazine, broadcast, website, or other outlet.

Praise for *Teacher in the Yellow House*

Luella Wagner pursues her gifts to teach in the classroom yet experiences disappointment, broken dreams, and not being seen for whom she truly is. It's inspiring, and guides the reader, when one feels called, to just keep turning up with an open and grateful heart.
— The Reverend Dr. Lauren Artress, author of *Walking a Sacred Path, Rediscovering the Labyrinth as a Spiritual Practice*

Author Luella Wagner's memoir *Teacher in the Yellow House* invites readers on a rare, stirring journey from Los Angeles Catholic schools to remote Montana. When teacher layoffs leave her adrift and struggling, Wagner trades her suburban condo for a tribal reservation, where she signs on to teach for one year. Her observational wit and open heart guide readers through the trials, misadventures, and ultimate joy she finds in her new surroundings and in herself.
— Cheryl Lubin Ph.D., J.D., Podcast Host of *In Our Times*, and Voiceover for *Bloom Where You Are Planted*

Born in Massachusetts, a stop off in Cali and a calling to Montana. Great read, full of ups and downs as a woman tries to find her calling on a reservation. A job move that turns into a spiritual destination.
— Mary Kennedy, Program Director, The Biz Studio, Los Angeles, CA

I loved this heartwarming story. I read it all in one session and could not put it down. It is a must for any teacher who is wondering if/how they matter, and will be an inspiration to anyone facing hard decisions.
— Diane Ventura, Co-Director (CEO) Teachers on Reserve, Glendale, CA

Luella's undefeatable humor shines through this memoir of her life-changing year living and teaching on a Montana Indian reservation.
— MB Kalis, Actress, SAG AFTRA, Voiceover for *Bloom Where You Are Planted*

Luella Wagner has been a dedicated teacher for many years at various locations throughout the world. A few years ago, she was given the opportunity to work in a Native American school on a reservation in Montana. It changed her life. This is the story of her journey from mainstream America to the culture and lives of our first peoples. As you read, you'll find yourself laughing and crying — sometimes simultaneously. Come with an open mind and an open heart and let her story change your life.
— Chris Machado, Executive Director, Holy Spirit Retreat Center, Encino, CA

It's hard to believe Luella taught for me some 30 years ago and we've been friends since then. She has more energy than the Energizer Bunny. Her love for kids is only surpassed by her love of God. She is an unbelievable, talented woman. I loved her show and I loved her book!
— Stephanie "Stevie" Connelly, Principal, Notre Dame High School (1997–2016), Sherman Oaks, CA

Luella Wagner's memoir provides a unique insight into the workings of a Native American reservation school. Wagner brings the reader into a world where students are challenged as never before. In the process she discovers her students' spark and as a result enkindles her own passion for teaching. A delightful read that will make you laugh and cry!
— Gina Finer, Principal, Immaculate Heart Middle School, Los Angeles, CA

TEACHER IN THE YELLOW HOUSE

My Year on a Montana Reservation

Luella Wagner

2024
Snow Crocus Publishing
Woodland Hills, California

Dedication

My memoir, *Teacher in the Yellow House*, is dedicated to Dolores Freeman, who drove me and my three cats, Tiger, Juanita, and Moo Moo fifteen hundred miles up to Montana so I could teach on an Indian reservation. At the end of the school year, she flew to Montana, picked up the U-Haul, drove out to the reservation and brought me and my three cats back to California. If it wasn't for her unselfishness and steadfast loyalty there would be no story. I am eternally grateful for her friendship.

TABLE OF CONTENTS

ACKNOWLEDGMENTS iii
FOREWORD vi
A NOTE TO THE READER 1
1 BLINDSIDED 2
2 WHY, WYOMING? 11
3 SHOW ME A SIGN 18
4 THE NATIVE SPIRIT LODGE 25
5 RING LAKE RANCH DID HAVE THE ANSWER 30
6 IS HEAT INCLUDED? 35
7 U-HAUL MY ASS 45
8 MY FIRST POWWOW 58
9 NATIVE AMERICAN WEEK 69
10 BATTLE OF LITTLE BIGHORN REVISITED 79
11 SWEAT LODGE 84
12 AMISH STORE 91
13 LEARNING TO LIVE WITHOUT 94
14 VERIZON ON THE HORIZON 98
15 THE GRASSHOPPER, THE LABRADOR, AND JD . 102
16 MY PHILOSOPHY OF EDUCATION 108
17 THE INDIAN WHO TAUGHT ME A LESSON 111
18 STAGE THREE 116
19 DEAD END 119
20 PICTURE DAY 123
21 PEACE PIPE 128
22 SNOW DAY 135
23 CHRISTMAS ON THE REZ 141
24 CABIN FEVER 145
25 TEACHER IN THE YELLOW HOUSE 150

26 RESERVATION BASKETBALL	155
27 BEADWORK	159
28 A THOUSAND CRANES	165
29 BLOOM WHERE YOU ARE PLANTED	168
30 FLIGHT OF THE BUTTERFLIES	174
31 WE SHALL SURVIVE	179
32 THANK YOU	186
33 SOME GOOD NEWS AND SOME SAD NEWS	192
34 A HAPPY ENDING	198
END NOTES	199

ACKNOWLEDGMENTS

It has been a long journey that started with a daily journal which led to presentations at numerous conferences at the local, state, and national levels which turned into a one-woman show at the Whitefire Theatre and now a published memoir. There have been many people along the way who have given me support, encouragement, and guidance and I would like to acknowledge them.

My cousin, Jim Little, encouraged me to keep a journal while I was on the reservation. I had no idea at the time how important his advice was. My journal became the basis for my lectures, my one-woman show, and now my memoir. I am so glad I took his advice.

Sister Chris Machado at Holy Spirit Retreat Center in Encino gave me the opportunity to present numerous retreats and workshops on Native American spirituality. Holy Spirit Retreat Center has been my refuge and source of inspiration as I have spent countless hours there writing my memoir.

Upon my return to California, the City of Angels Kateri Circle welcomed me into their community and allowed me to share in their rich spiritual tradition. Eva Walters, Founder of the City of Angels Kateri Circle, has had a profound impact on the direction of my life. I am sincerely grateful to her.

Bryan Rasmussen, Artistic Director of the Whitefire Theatre in Sherman Oaks, gave me the opportunity to perform my show *Bloom Where You Are Planted* about my time living and teaching on the reservation. The show allowed me to tell my story to a live audience and gain positive feedback while at the same time giving me the inspiration to write my memoir.

Adele Field has guided my writing the past few years as an incredibly gifted and talented editor. I would not be a writer if it wasn't for her constant support and encouragement. More importantly she has been my confidant and loyal friend in time of need.

Greg Baldwin, comedian and actor, inspired me with his kind and encouraging words during the final stages of my writing.

Sadly many of those who had a direct and lasting impact on my life during my time on the reservation have passed away. It is my intention to honor their memory. They are:

Marian Finn, loyal friend and fellow teacher, followed me through all the stages of my career. She even came to visit me on the reservation for the holidays.

Leonard Muggee was my accountant and my tax advisor for several years. In addition to providing me with sound financial advice he always gave me lasting "life" advice which was worth so much more. He is dearly missed.

Jim Fowler was a theologian, Harvard professor, and author of *Stages of Faith*. My chance encounter with him was a sign that I was onto something big and all I needed was a little bit of faith to make it happen.

Carl Koch was the Director of the Ring Lake Ranch in Wyoming and Editor of St. Mary's Press. He provided me with the means to go to the Ring Lake Ranch and he had total confidence in my ability to know God's will. His generosity and kindness will always be remembered.

Eufemia Jacob, Ph.D., RN, Associate Professor of Nursing at UCLA, prepared me in so many ways for the cold Montana winter ahead. In addition to providing me bedding, blankets, and bathrobes, she also provided me with the emotional support I needed to get to the reservation.

Father Paschal was the holiest man I had ever met. His gentle and humble spirit permeated the entire campus. His quiet demeanor and gratitude for life was a constant inspiration to me.

George Yves de Seve and Edie Charlotte de Seve were the most loving couple I had ever encountered. They encouraged me to go to the reservation and they welcomed me when I came back. Their love for me was truly a blessing.

Ken Kania was one of the most dedicated teachers I had ever known. His wealth of knowledge and his undeterred patience was a model for every teacher.

Father Emmett, also known as Soaring Eagle, had the rare combination of compassion and financial acumen. His love for the Cheyenne people and his ability to raise funds turned a floundering school into the academic institution that it is today. He saved the school and me.

Lee Lone Bear was a spiritual leader, a traditional healer, and a devout Catholic. He demonstrated the complementary natures of Native American spirituality and Catholicism. His powerful presence will always be felt.

Charles Little Old Man was a Sacred Hat Keeper and played a major role in numerous Sundance ceremonies. He lived and taught the spiritual traditions of the Cheyenne people. He will never be forgotten.

Lou Pavek, 1950s graduate of St. Labre, played a key role in the students' documentary, *We Shall Survive*. We are eternally grateful for his contribution.

FOREWORD

Luella Wagner makes a difference.

Luella is the type of educator that any school would be blessed to have. As she humbly recounts throughout this book, Luella consistently shows personal dedication and educational creativity in order to reach her students. She possesses the perseverance to allow this creativity to work its wonders. Luella is able to do this not simply because she engages with her students relentlessly. She does this with the faith that the Lord is with her. Luella is not afraid to look silly or be misunderstood by the self-righteous. She knows what ultimately matters is that students learn.

Luella is comforted by the knowledge that she is a humble instrument of the Lord. I witnessed this reality the few years Luella was my colleague at the high school where we taught together before she taught at Santa Maria de las Rosas High School. Tragically for Santa Maria de las Rosas, her excellence was not recognized and appreciated. The shock of having your vocation being taken from you is one that often drives one to cynicism. Yet Luella refused to dwell on the negative and had confidence the Lord is always there for everyone, especially those in distress. That is the reason she was drawn to the Montana reservation.

Obstacles are opportunities for Luella. This book is a joy for those who seek to make a positive difference and are willing to trust forces larger than themselves to affect the world in a positive way.

— Richard Woolery, Social Science Educator

A NOTE TO THE READER

This is the story of my experience living and teaching at a little-known school in Ashland, Montana called St. Labre Indian Mission School. Who was Saint Labre, anyway?

In the early years of my career, I vaguely remember entertaining the idea of teaching on an Indian reservation, but it was only a dashing thought that quickly vanished. Instead, my life took me to South America where I taught for several years and then to American Samoa for a short teaching stint. Returning to California, I thought my rambling days were over until twenty years later the notion of teaching on an Indian Reservation became a reality. No longer in my youth and unwilling to make a drastic lifestyle change, I accepted the inevitable and packed up my belongings and my cats and headed to St. Labre Indian Mission School. I hope my story inspires and encourages others who are facing difficult decisions and that they may find the courage to go where their destiny calls them.

A few things before you journey with me to Montana.

When I arrived on the reservation, I was very diligent to say Native American rather than Indian, however I noticed that many of those living on the reservation would refer to themselves as Indian. One day I asked the human resources director at my school if I should use Native American or Indian and she said, "We're Indians, but if you want to say Native American that's fine too." So I use both terms interchangeably throughout the memoir.

As for Indian names, I encountered a number of variations in capitalization and spacing. I have referenced all Native American names as they were recorded in my attendance/grade book and school newsletters or brochures.

All scripture verses were taken from the New International Version.

CHAPTER ONE

BLINDSIDED

I never saw it coming.

It started as a typical sunny Southern California day. I drove to work along the same crowded freeway as I had done for the past two years. I listened to the *Mark and Brian Show* as I did every morning, gearing up for another day of teaching. It was the end of the school year and I was excited about summer and a trip I had planned to Wyoming. Little did I know that my life was about to be turned upside down.

In just a few short months I would find myself living in a different state, a different time zone, a different climate, and an entirely different culture.

I had been teaching at Santa Maria de las Rosas High School for two years. I loved my job. I had a great rapport with my students and I got along well with the teachers and staff. There were one or two people who could be a bit of a pain, but no matter where you go there's always going to be something, right? So I just accepted it. It was an easy commute. I had a decent classroom and I was done writing resumes. I planned on staying at the school until I retired, in about another twenty years or so, but things don't always work out the way you plan.

The week before, I had celebrated Mother's Day with my good friend Marian. Neither one of us had kids of our own, but we had taught and nurtured thousands of other peoples' kids, not to mention a number of stray cats that had crossed our paths. We unabashedly celebrated each Mother's Day with flowers, a champagne brunch, and good conversation, and this year I was feeling especially confident about my future.

I happily commented to Marian, "I plan on staying at Santa Maria de las Rosas High School until I retire."

My classroom was a work of art — my students' art. It had taken me two years to build it up. I had their pictures, drawings, and photos arranged perfectly on the walls. Students had stenciled positive words like Happiness, Spontaneity, Excitement, Compassion, and stapled them to the ceiling. Yes, even the ceiling was a work of art. In the back of my classroom I had a media center with video equipment and cameras alongside a magazine section. We had homework parties after school where students could do their homework, listen to music, and meet with their friends. I wanted to give my students a positive, lasting memory of being in my classroom.

On Mondays and Tuesdays I taught directly from the book, so no one could accuse me of not covering the curriculum. I was one of those teachers who could teach without a book, tapping into students' creativity while at the same time covering the material in a fun and memorable way. That type of instruction usually makes administrators nervous, so I used the textbook to keep them happy. On Wednesdays, Thursdays, and Fridays, I chose activities that allowed my students to use their own imaginations, while at the same time providing solid direction with high expectations. I assigned projects that required students to write and produce their own videos based on the material being studied. I introduced photography as a tool to capture specific moments that reflected the lesson objectives. What the students cherished most was the meditation at the start of every class. We would take a few moments of silence to quiet ourselves down, focus our attention, and tap into our muse. They loved it! In addition to classroom activities, I invited entertaining and inspiring guest speakers to talk to my classes. I arranged for students to go on fun yet educational field trips. Every day was creative, informative, and dynamic. It was the culmination of eighteen years of teaching; knowing what worked and what didn't. It was my best teaching.

There was nothing out of the ordinary about this particular day. I had no gut feeling that something pivotal was about to happen. Late in the afternoon, as I was sitting at my desk scrolling through my emails and waiting for the last student to leave my classroom, I noticed an email from the principal asking me to see him the next morning. I never get called to the principal's office. I immediately went into a panic. It's never good when you are called to the principal's office whether you are a student or a teacher.

I immediately rushed over to my department chair and asked why I was being called to the office.

"You need to talk to the principal."

Ah, yes, the principal. My assessment was that he was more suited for a game show host or a cruise director than a high school administrator. Most of his energy was directed toward rallies, sports events, and school dances. I got the impression that he wasn't that interested in academics. He never once observed my classroom. My department chair was of the same ilk; no teaching credentials, very little teaching experience, and limited communication skills. He could barely run a department meeting, let alone a department. He spent most of his time cutting out coupons for fast food restaurants and taping them to the campus ministry door with a sign that read "Please take." When he wasn't clipping coupons he was watering the plants outside his office. He didn't have a teaching background, but he was a priest, and that's how he wound up as department chair at Santa Maria de las Rosas High School. These two people were my supervisors.

I needed answers. I raced over to the vice principal's office. I trusted him completely. He had observed my classroom teaching twice and each time I received a positive evaluation. If he knew anything, he would tell me. Luckily, he was in his office. I stuck my head in and asked if he had a few minutes. He must have seen the panic in my face because he waved for me to come in right away.

I tried to remain calm and cool. "I got an email to see the principal tomorrow morning. Do you know anything about this?"

He looked at me, stunned. "No, I don't. No one has mentioned a word to me about this."

"Am I getting fired tomorrow?"

"I don't know if you are going to get fired or not," he said, "but by law they have to tell you by Friday if you are going to be given a contract or not for the next year."

Tomorrow was Thursday. It was all too close. I felt my world was about to come crashing down and there was nothing I could do except go through the motions as best I could.

That night I stopped by my friend Dolores' house. We had been friends for almost three decades. I met her when I first moved to California while we were both working at the Hilton Hotel in Burbank. Even though our lives had taken us on completely different paths over the years, we always remained close. Now we were living in the same condominium complex, but in different buildings. It was good to have a friend close by, especially in times like this. Immediately, she could tell that something wasn't right.

"What happened?"

"I think I'm going to get fired tomorrow."

Dolores brushed it off, "Oh, c'mon. They're not going to fire you."

"Oh, yes, they are."

"Why would you even think that?"

Trying to stay composed, I said, "I got an email from the principal today to meet him in his office tomorrow morning. They have until the end of this week to tell me if I'm going to be given a contract or not for the next year."

Dolores still wasn't convinced. "You're overreacting. You always think the worst. The principal isn't going to fire you. He's probably going to tell you what a great job you're doing."

I rolled my eyes. "Dolores, principals don't do things like that. They call you in to tell you that a parent complained or you're giving out too many As or too many Fs, but they never call you in to tell you that you're doing a good job."

"Are you sure you're not just imagining things?"

"I am not imagining things. I am predicting things. I am going to get fired tomorrow."

I left Dolores' house with a sickening feeling welling up inside of me.

That night I couldn't sleep. My heart raced. With 12% unemployment, my job prospects were bleak. Public schools were not hiring. They were actually handing out layoff notices. They weren't even hiring for substitute teachers. As for Catholic schools, I had eighteen years of experience, a teaching credential, and a Master's degree, but Catholic school administrators would rather hire someone straight out of college with no experience than pay for a veteran teacher with my qualifications. I envisioned myself homeless, living under the bridge with my three cats, Tiger, Juanita, and Moo Moo. I tossed and turned all night.

The next morning I sat outside the principal's office. It was torture. After a few minutes, which seemed like hours, the principal's assistant led me into his office. I politely sat down and reminded myself to stay calm.

I waited for the principal to start the conversation, but he didn't. So I began by telling him about all the projects I was working on. Without any hesitation he said, "We are not going to offer you a contract for next year. And we don't have to give you any reason, because it's written in your contract that we don't have to give you a reason. But in case you want to know, your department chair doesn't have confidence in your ability to teach."

The idea was absurd. I had more teaching experience and better qualifications than my department chair. Throughout my entire career, no one had ever accused me of not being able to teach. I walked out of the principal's office in a daze. Even though I had anticipated it, I was still in shock. I didn't know how I was going to go back into my classroom and teach for the rest of the day, let alone the rest of the year, but somehow I managed. As upset as I was, I didn't show it. I didn't want to say or do anything that I would later regret.

The reality began to sink in. In a few short weeks, I would have no money coming in. The archdiocese does not contribute to unemployment insurance so I couldn't file a claim. No severance package either, which is an interesting policy coming from an organization that preaches social justice to everyone else. But it's all in the way you look at it. It's one of those opportunities in the Catholic Church for practicing your faith. No unemployment, no severance, no golden parachutes — all you can do is hope and pray that a miracle will happen before you go splat on the concrete.

I went home that day and plopped down on the couch, staring up at the ceiling as if the ceiling contained all of life's answers. I posed the perennial question that everyone asks at times like these. "Why? Why is this happening? Why me?" The idea that some priest could get me fired because he didn't think I could teach was so wrong, but deep down I felt this inkling that God was doing something really big in my life. He just forgot to tell me about it.

The vice principal encouraged me to reach out to the superintendent, the Monsignor, and ask for a meeting to discuss the situation. I sent him an email and left a message on his phone, and the answer I got back from his assistant was, "The Monsignor will have nothing to do with you." Those were the exact words. I remember it like it was yesterday. It felt like a knife in the gut.

Dolores told me to tell my students that my contract was not being renewed, but I knew that if I caused a commotion I could jeopardize my chance with a potential employer who could call the school for a reference. So I kept quiet.

As I saw it, I had three options. One was to fight it. I could have told my students to stage a walkout in protest or to tell their parents to call the archdiocese and flood them with complaints, but something stopped me from doing that. If I was reinstated, I would have to stay at Santa Maria de las Rosas High School forever and that wasn't really such a great idea since they didn't want me there to begin with. My second option was to brood about it. I could keep it inside for years and pretend that it didn't bother me and then after ten years of bitter resentment be diagnosed with kidney stones or heart disease or even worse, premature death. Then there was my third option. In a strange sort of way I wanted to know what was behind Door #3. Remember that game show, *Let's Make a Deal* where a contestant was given something of value that could be traded for something behind one of the doors onstage? It could either be something of greater value or a dud. That was the risk you took. Well, I knew what Santa Maria de las Rosas High School had to offer and I was willing to accept the "prickly thorns" of the situation in the hopes that I would gain something far greater than what I had. I decided I would go for Door #3 having no idea what was behind it.

The last week of school was the hardest. The only thing that got me through it was the prayer of Mother Teresa, the one she kept on her wall and I kept on mine:

People are often unreasonable, illogical and self-centered; forgive them anyway.

If you are kind, people may accuse you of selfish, ulterior motives; be kind anyway.

If you are successful, you will win some false friends and some true enemies; succeed anyway.

If you are honest and frank, people may cheat you; be honest and frank anyway.

What you spend years building, someone could destroy overnight; build anyway.

If you find serenity and happiness, they may be jealous; be happy anyway.

The good you do today, people will often forget tomorrow; do good anyway.

Give the world the best you have, and it may never be enough; give the world the best you've got anyway.

You see, in the final analysis, it is between you and God; it never was between you and them anyway.

The part of the prayer that stuck out was: *What you spend years building, someone could destroy overnight; build anyway.*

As I finished clearing out my classroom and packing up my few belongings, I repeated over and over again, "What you spend years building, someone could destroy overnight; build anyway."

Eighteen years of teaching, and it all came crashing down in an instant.

I never let on to the students that I was leaving. I knew they would have questions and I didn't want to create any hullabaloo on my way out the door. I knew they would be upset. Or maybe it was sheer embarrassment on my part, but I just thought it would be better if I left quietly.

I did ask one student, Andrew, for his email. I made it sound very nonchalant. Like, "Hey, let's stay in touch over the summer." I knew eventually I would tell him what happened and he could pass it along to the rest of the class.

On the last day of school one of my most loyal students came in to see me. Since most of my classroom had been torn down she asked the obvious, "Ms. Wagner, are you coming back next year?"

Holding back my tears, I said, "No, I'm not, Maria. They don't want me back."

She was devastated. "Oh, Ms. Wagner, I am so sorry. I am so sorry."

"I am too, Maria. I am too." And then we hugged each other.

On the last day of school I found a stack of gift cards from Starbucks, Trader Joe's, and Target on my desk with a few candy bars, and cards from the teachers. I knew it was their way of saying, "sorry" and that they wished me the best. I appreciated their kindness. So what if I got fired for no reason and I couldn't collect unemployment and I wasn't given a severance package? I could still get a chai latte at Starbucks. Priceless.

CHAPTER TWO

WHY, WYOMING?

There was one bright spot in all of this. A month earlier as I sat in the office of my tax adviser anticipating a big refund, I said, "Once I get my refund, you know where I want to go?"

Without looking up from his computer, Leonard asked, "Where?"

"Bhutan. I really want to go to Bhutan."

"Bhutan? Where's that?"

"It's in Asia, below China and above Bangladesh."

"Why would you want to go there?"

"When I was in India two years ago, I met this guy who went to Bhutan and he said it was life-changing. And that's what I want. I want something life-changing. How much money am I getting back? Enough to go to Bhutan?"

I had known Leonard for years. He was more than a tax advisor, he was a spiritual advisor as well. Every year in addition to doing my tax returns, Leonard would give me some sort of spiritual direction. This year was no different. Leonard posed the proposition, "Why don't you go to Wyoming?"

"Wyoming? Why would I go to Wyoming? C'mon Leonard, you know me better than that. I go to places like India, Brazil, Russia, not Wyoming. I can't even believe you said that."

"You don't have to travel to the other side of the planet to have a life-changing experience. You can do that right here in this country. I am only suggesting that you go to Wyoming and see what it has to offer instead of traveling halfway around the world. There are many beautiful places right here in this country that you haven't even seen yet and Wyoming is one of them. I think you would love it there."

"What on earth would I do there?"

Leonard, sat back from his computer, turned towards me, lowered his head and peered above the rim of his glasses and said, "I don't know. You'll have to figure that out for yourself."

It was obvious from his office pictures that Leonard was a frontier man. He spent half his time in Los Angeles during tax season and the other half in Wyoming, fishing. His suggestion to go to Wyoming was projection, but he did spark my curiosity. When I got home I googled vacation spots in Wyoming and I found a place called the Ring Lake Ranch. Set in the mountains, surrounded by lakes and wildlife, the Ring Lake Ranch offered hiking, horseback riding, bird-watching, and kayaking. In addition, there were nightly discussion groups led by academics covering a wide range of topics. I took Leonard's advice and decided to go to Wyoming. I called the Ring Lake Ranch and made a reservation for one week in June. But now that I had lost my job, I couldn't justify spending the money. Even with a tax refund, I had to hold on to every penny until I got another job, so I called the ranch to cancel my reservation.

A warm-hearted voice answered the phone which made it even harder for me to cancel my stay. "Hi, my name is Luella Wagner and I had a reservation for the week of June 13th. I've had something unexpected come up and I'm going to have to cancel."

"Oh, no! I'm so sorry," the voice on the other end of the phone said. She sounded so sincere and even though I didn't have to, I felt obligated to tell her the reason why I wouldn't be able to go to the ranch.

So I said rather embarrassedly, "Yeah, I lost my job. It was totally unexpected and I really can't justify spending any money on a vacation right now."

There was a pause and then she said, "Luella, you need to come to the Ring Lake Ranch now more than ever. Don't worry about the cost, Carl will give you a scholarship. All you have to do is find a way to get here."

"Who's Carl?"

"Carl runs the ranch and… he's my husband."

I couldn't believe it. "Really? I can stay at the Ring Lake Ranch for free?"

"Yes, and if you come to the Ring Lake Ranch you will find the answers you are looking for." Spoken like a true prophet.

This was too good a deal to pass up. I couldn't believe my good fortune. Now I had to go to the Ring Lake Ranch. There was something very mysterious calling me to Wyoming. I actually believed her when she said I would find the answers I was looking for.

Once school got out, I headed up to Wyoming. With my tax refund, I was able to pay for a round trip airline ticket from Los Angeles to Utah and then rent a car for the drive to the ranch from Salt Lake City. Leonard was right. Wyoming was beautiful.

On the way up I made one very important stop. I had just passed through Lander, Wyoming when I saw a sign for Sacajawea's gravesite. I knew that I would never be through these parts again, so I took a slight detour to the Sacajawea Cemetery, Fort Washakie on the Wind River Indian Reservation. It took me a while to locate her grave, but once I did, I got out of the car and paid my respects.

I reminisced back twenty years when my seventh grade students dramatized great heroes in U.S. History and Sacajawea was one of them. I met up with one of my students years later and she told me, "Ms. Wagner you gave me the part of Sacajawea and that is the only thing I remember from seventh grade!" Well, at least she remembered that!

Coming out of the cemetery, I lost my sense of direction, took a wrong turn and ended up not knowing which way I was headed. I made a couple of U-turns hoping to get back to the main road, but I just seemed to be going in circles. I found myself on a lonely, deserted road with a few houses spotting the landscape. My cell phone didn't work in the area and I didn't have a GPS. I had to do the old-fashioned thing and ask someone for directions. The only problem was, no one was around.

Houses were somewhat scattered along the road every quarter mile or so. I eventually pulled into a random driveway, got out of the car, walked up to the door and rang the doorbell. An Indian came to the door, which made sense since I was on a reservation. I told him I went to the cemetery and somehow I got lost and I needed to get back to the main road. At first he just stared at me. I guess he wasn't used to a lost white woman knocking on his door asking for directions. He looked at me and then pointed his finger.

"That's the direction I should take to get back to the main road?"

He nodded his head.

"Just follow that road?" I asked, pointing in the same direction that he did.

He nodded his head again.

I took his advice and finally got back to Route 287. At the time, I didn't realize how prophetic those two stops along the way would be — a visit to Sacajawea's gravesite and an Indian pointing me in the right direction.

It was another hour drive before I reached Dubois and just as the sun was about to set, I saw the sign for the Ring Lake Ranch. I followed a dirt road that twisted and turned for about a mile and a half until I pulled into a parking lot for what appeared to be the main lodge. I grabbed my suitcase and headed down the path that led to the lodge. I knew I was a bit late, but I thought I could just sneak in and no one would notice. I tried to open the door very quietly. Just as I made my stealth entrance, forty heads turned and stared in my direction. It was obvious that the retreat had already begun and I was the last one to arrive.

I was a bit embarrassed to say the least. When I apologized for being late I was greeted with one of the warmest welcomes I had ever received. People were tripping over themselves to find a chair and make room for me. The energy in the room was positive, powerful, and electrifying. My daylong journey from Los Angeles brought me to a treasure chest that hopefully was filled with the answers I was looking for.

That night I settled in to my "cabin in the woods." Being in Wyoming was good for me. A change of scenery made all the difference in the world. I decided that for the next few days I was not going to think about the fact that I was unemployed. I wasn't going to worry about paying the bills. I wasn't going to worry about my cats. My friend Lynn would check in on them every day and feed them so I knew they were in good hands. I wasn't even going to entertain the crazy notion that I might end up homeless in a couple of weeks. Instead I would enjoy every moment at the Ring Lake Ranch. I would immerse myself in the daily activities and the nightly seminars. I would engage in good conversation with whoever wanted to talk to me and most importantly, I would make time to relax while waiting patiently for answers.

The next morning, there was a huge breakfast buffet in the dining hall with eggs, omelets, waffles, choice of cereals, mounds of fresh fruit, and a variety of breads and pastries. As I made my way through the line, a woman approached me and asked if I was by myself. When I told her I was, she kindly invited me to join her family. She was there with her father, mother, husband, and two kids. I sat down next to her father who she introduced as Jim.

Jim looked at me and asked, "So, where are you from?"

"Well, I live in California, but I'm originally from Massachusetts." Even though I had lived in California for twenty years, I still had an East Coast accent. So whenever someone asked me where I was from, I would revert back to my Massachusetts roots.

And then he asked, "Where did you go to college?"

"Boston University."

Jim chuckled, "I used to teach across the river."

That could only mean one of two things — MIT or Harvard, so I asked, "MIT or Harvard?"

"I taught at Harvard."

"Really? What did you teach?"

"Theology. And when I wasn't teaching at Harvard, I used to go over to Boston College and teach those nuns and priests a thing or two." I knew one priest he could have taught a thing or two! I was sitting next to Jim Fowler, noted theologian and author of *Stages of Faith*. It was a truly memorable conversation for me. And what were the chances?

It was a packed week, for sure. Carole, the hike leader, pointed out ancient Native American petroglyphs as she led us along the hiking trails. On the days that I didn't go hiking, I went horseback riding. I hadn't ridden a horse in years and at the end of the day, my legs were sore, but my mind had shifted and I suddenly felt a burst of confidence that I hadn't felt in quite a long time. Horses do that. In addition to hiking and horseback riding we went into town for an evening of square dancing.

There was an intellectual side to all of this as well. Maggie Edson, who won the Pulitzer Prize for her play, *Wit*, led intensive workshops that included engaging topics, insightful discussions, and interactive role play. During one session, she actually called me up on stage for an impromptu dialogue between a historical commentator and Josephus. Maggie played the part of the commentator and I played the part of Josephus. I made everybody laugh and it's a good feeling when you can make people laugh.

After five days my time on the ranch came to an end. As I packed my bags and headed out to my car, I thought to myself, 'this has been a great experience, but I didn't find the answers I was looking for.' I was going back to Los Angeles with absolutely no idea what I was supposed to do with my life.

Before I left the ranch, I made one last stop at the office to thank Carl. I told him that I was a bit scared going back to Los Angeles without any job prospects, but he told me not to worry that something would come up. 'Easy for him to say,' I thought, but in a few short weeks, his words would ring prophetically true. Subtle events, chance meetings, and random encounters were already leading me along the path to the most difficult yet rewarding experience of my life.

CHAPTER THREE

SHOW ME A SIGN

Back in Los Angeles, I applied for jobs all over the country — Texas, Washington D.C., Washington state, Oregon, Florida, New York. I don't even know what possessed me to do this. I guess I instinctively knew that I was meant to leave California. I even applied for a teaching job at a small Indian school in southeastern Montana. After a few days, I got a reply back. You've got to be kidding me! All those resumes and cover letters I sent out and the only reply I got back was from an Indian reservation in Montana? I didn't answer the email and I continued my search.

In the meantime, I did get a part-time job working at Kiddie Kandids in Calabasas. It has since gone out of business. I took pictures of little kids and then I had to convince their parents to buy the most expensive photo package we offered. While I was grateful for the job, there had to be something better out there for me to do. But I wasn't getting any callbacks except for that one Indian school and no way was I going to trade sunny Southern California for freezing cold Montana. I never even wanted to fly over Montana, let alone go and live there, but I couldn't survive on eight bucks an hour at Kiddie Kandids.

I'm not sure if it was desperation or curiosity or a combination of both, but I decided to do a little research. I got online and searched for apartments in Montana. I was pleasantly surprised. I found several apartments that were affordable, roomy, relatively new, or recently remodeled. I had never been to that part of the country before and for a split second I actually entertained the thought of living in Montana. Then I snapped back at myself, 'What are you thinking! Stop it! Get those thoughts out of your head right now! You are not going to Montana!' But the apartments were really cute and sometimes it can be fun setting up a new home. Then I realized the huge mistake I had made. While looking for an apartment online I had used the state abbreviation MO, thinking that was Montana. No! That is the abbreviation for Missouri! The abbreviation for Montana is MT. When I searched for an apartment in Montana where the school was located there was nothing. I couldn't find a single apartment for rent anywhere near the school. 'Where did the teachers live? Where did the students and their families live?' I wondered. It was a mystery and even though I had no intentions of going there, I was curious as to where people in the area lived. I did find a couple of apartments in Colstrip about forty-five miles away, but I just couldn't see myself commuting to and from the Indian reservation ninety miles round-trip every day. No, this was not the direction for me to go in. I was going down the wrong path.

Besides, I had to think about my cats. Tiger, Juanita, and Moo Moo were from Southern California. They wouldn't like Montana. The climate was too cold for cats. Did they even have cats in Montana? I couldn't imagine stray cats living in Montana in the freezing cold. I actually googled cat shelters in Montana and called one of them up.

"Hello there, I have a few questions."

"Sure, what would you like to know?"

"Um"… I hesitated and then I said, "I was just wondering, do you have lots of cats in Montana?"

"Oh, yes, we have a lot of cats in Montana," the woman on the phone replied. She was a real cat person, I could tell.

"I'm from California and I'm thinking about moving to Montana with my three cats and I'm really worried about them living in the cold climate."

"Your cats will be fine as long as you never let them out of the house." She was so pleasant and willing to spend time talking to me about my cats that I felt I could be really honest with her.

"They are used to Southern California and I'm worried that it's going to be really cold up there."

"We have heat. It's not Antarctica!" She made me laugh.

Another question, "Do you think they will be able to make the trip up there?"

"Of course. Cats do really well when they travel long distances." She reassured me.

"If I have more questions, can I call you back?"

"Of course, you can."

When I hung up the phone I had a really good feeling about Montana.

Then I did the unthinkable. I checked out the school's website. It was a colorful website with pictures of Indians and information about the school with a list of the faculty and staff, but I couldn't tell what the classrooms were like. I envisioned myself teaching in a trailer with no heat, wearing a goose down parka, pointing to some arbitrary fact on the board with a bunch of students who were distant and disinterested. No, this wasn't going to work. This was a crazy idea and I couldn't believe that I had already given it this much thought, but this was the only school in the entire country that was even interested in what I had to offer. They kept sending me emails with possible interview dates.

I needed advice, badly. I had to talk this over with someone; someone who would come at this from a different perspective. I called my good friend Ray and we decided to meet for lunch in Marina Del Rey. Ray lived in Torrance, a city about twenty miles south of Los Angeles, while I lived in Woodland Hills about twenty-five miles northwest of Los Angeles. Marina Del Rey was the halfway point for both of us. Ray suggested that we meet for lunch at Islands, a trendy burger and fries hangout with burger names like Maui, Big Wave, Hawaiian, and Malibu, and for me the Veggie.

At the time, I had no idea how significant driving to that location would be in predicting my life's trajectory.

Ray was the host of his own talk show on a local television station. He had been my instructor a few years back when I enrolled in a broadcast journalism class at UCLA. Each week we would work in pairs and role play our interviews while Ray provided valuable feedback. The class had proved beneficial a few years later when I taught a course in broadcast journalism at Daniel Murphy Catholic High School.

When the class ended, Ray and I stayed in touch and every so often we would get together for lunch or coffee and give each other an update on what was going on in our lives. I was really curious as to what Ray's thoughts would be about me going to Montana.

"So, what's been going on?" Ray asked.

"I lost my job."

"Aww, sorry to hear that. Do you know what you are going to do yet?"

"I'm thinking about taking a teaching job in Montana."

"Montana! Why would you go all the way to Montana for a job? Can't you get a teaching job here in LA?"

"Ray, I called every single school district in the area and they're not hiring. They're not even hiring for substitute teachers. I sent out resumes all over the country and this is the only school that wants me."

"Where in Montana?"

"Northern Cheyenne Indian Reservation."

"An Indian reservation!!! I can't see you living on an Indian reservation in Montana. You're a city person. I don't think you can survive in the wilderness."

"Yeah," I said, "but this will give me the opportunity to experience Native American culture and tradition. I love learning about different cultures. That's why I spent three years in Brazil and a year in American Samoa. It's not that farfetched. I don't have kids or a husband. I can pick up and go anytime I want."

I munched down my veggie burger while Ray shook his head.

"You've really given this some thought, haven't you?"

"Yeah, I have."

"I just can't see you moving to Montana. It's too cold up there. You'll freeze to death."

"I used to live in Massachusetts and I know what the cold is, I can handle it."

I couldn't even believe those words were coming out of my mouth. The main reason why I left Massachusetts was to get out of the cold. I still remember that blistering cold day in January 1982 as I walked across the Charles River Bridge. I was bundled up in layers upon layers, but the wind still penetrated my bones. Right then and there I thought to myself, 'I've got to get the hell out of here' and I headed to Southern California. Ray was right. I wouldn't last through a Montana winter.

While I finished off my burger, Ray reiterated, "It's just not you."

"I know it's not me, but nobody else wants me."

"You'll find a job here. You don't have to go all the way to Montana for a job. You? In Montana? What a crazy idea!"

"Yeah, you're right. It is a crazy idea."

Ray walked me out to my car and gave me one last bit of advice. "Forget about Montana. You don't want to leave Southern California. Just be patient. Something will come up."

I got in my car and headed back to the Valley. Ray was right. I would find a job here in Southern California.

But as I was driving up the 405 freeway, I still didn't feel right. I didn't feel right about going to Montana and I didn't feel right about not going to Montana. And then out of total desperation, I said one of those prayers that we have all said at one time or another. "God, if you want me to go to Montana… if it's Your will for me to go to Montana… just give me a sign …" And then I added, "Make it so obvious that I won't have any doubts at all that You're calling me to Montana."

Right after I said that prayer, right smack in front of me, I saw the sign, MONTANA AVE EXIT. "Oh, no! That sign doesn't count! I said make it obvious. That was too obvious." Anxiety raced through my mind. "Oh my God! I can't believe I saw that sign." I had passed that sign a million times and it never meant anything. I felt like I had been hit with a 2x4.

I tried to convince myself that it wasn't an answer to prayer, it was just a bizarre coincidence. My prayers don't get answered that fast. Plus, I could never admit to something like that. If anyone asked me, "Why did you go to Montana?" and I said, "Oh, well I was driving on the 405 freeway and I asked God to give me a sign and right after that I saw the sign MONTANA AVE EXIT and that's why I went to Montana," they would think I was nuts. No one in their right mind would make a momentous decision like moving out of state based on a sign they saw on the freeway.

I asked, "Why? Why? Why did I even notice that sign? Why did I even say that prayer? Can we just forget that I said that prayer?"

I didn't even know who I was talking to. I tried to blot it out of my mind. 'Just pretend you never saw that sign,' I told myself. Once I made my way onto the 101 freeway I thought I would feel better, but it still bothered me. 'I can't believe I saw that sign!' Now I was in a total state of panic and confusion. And then I thought, 'I know. I will talk to Grey Wolf. He'll tell me what to do.'

CHAPTER FOUR

THE NATIVE SPIRIT LODGE

A few years before, I had taught a class in world religions and one of the units was on Native American spirituality. While I was somewhat familiar with Native American history and culture, I knew very little about their spiritual beliefs and practices. Fortunately for me, there was a new store in my neighborhood called The Native Spirit Lodge. The store carried dream catchers, tumbled rocks, crystals, shells, deer antlers, totem poles, incense, and so much more.

I loved it from the minute I walked in. The store was a hub of interesting people and they all seemed to gravitate to one person, Grey Wolf. He was originally from Canada, a member of the Cree tribe, and owner of the store. He was tall, with long grey hair and piercing blue eyes. He was soft-spoken and had a warm, gentle spirit. He taught me many things about Native American culture and tradition. He explained the smudging ceremony. He shared his experience of the vision quest. He told me many stories of Indigenous peoples. He was a great resource for my class and even though my class in world religions ended, our friendship continued.

I already knew what he was going to say if I told him I was thinking about going to work on an Indian reservation. He would say something like, "Hey, that's great! You've always wanted to learn about Native American culture and now you have the chance to live on a reservation! That's fantastic. I am so happy for you."

Yeah, that was it. He would say something like that and that would give me the motivation I needed to go to Montana.

When I walked into his shop, Grey Wolf was busy with a customer, so I just walked around, looking again for a sign, maybe one not so conspicuous this time, or maybe one that screamed out at me STAY IN CALIFORNIA. I strolled around the store and then I saw it, another sign — a poster staring straight at me; the same poster that hung in my classroom for years. It was a nice poster, but I never really paid that much attention to the inscription on the bottom. It was a picture of a Native American on horseback with hands outstretched embracing the Great Plains ahead of him and in the clouds was a vision of a buffalo. The poster read:

Face the future with an open heart…

Seek new experiences with an open mind…

Embrace your destiny with open arms.

Oh, noooooooooo! I didn't want to embrace my destiny. I didn't want any edifying growth experience. I just wanted a job so I could pay my bills.

Finally, Grey Wolf came over to me. "How are you? I haven't seen you for a while. What's going on?"

"Oh Grey Wolf, I just lost my job. That's all."

"Oh, that just means that something better will come along."

"Yeah, I know. That's what I wanted to talk to you about. I am thinking about taking a job on an Indian reservation in Montana."

Grey Wolf looked at me, puzzled, "Montana? What reservation?"

"Northern Cheyenne. It's up by the Little Bighorn Battlefield. In a little tiny town called Ashland. Do you know it?"

He said nothing.

"Yeah, I am really thinking about going. I mean I would learn so much about the culture. I would be right there living on an Indian reservation."

He looked at me. "Doing what?"

"Teaching. Yeah, I'm actually thinking about doing it. What do you think?"

He said nothing.

"Well, what do you think?" I asked.

"Don't go," he said.

"What?" I was shocked. "Don't go? Grey Wolf, I thought you would be the one person encouraging me to go. I've been coming in here for years talking to you about Native American culture and spirituality. I thought you would be like, 'Hey, go for it!'"

Grey Wolf looked at me and said, "I'm from Canada. Why do you think I moved down here? It's freezing up there."

I couldn't believe the next words coming out of my mouth. "I know what the cold is like. I grew up in Massachusetts. I can take it." I was opening up my big fat mouth again. Why did I keep doing that?

Grey Wolf looked at me, "Do you know how cold it gets in Montana? The temperatures go below zero. C'mon, you love Southern California. You don't want to leave here, do you?"

"You're right. I don't want to leave Los Angeles, but I can't find a job here."

"What's the school?"

I admitted that it was a Catholic school.

Grey Wolf had told me some stories about Catholic schools on the reservations and how they had mistreated the Indians in the past, but I was sure this school wasn't like that. I said, "I can pull it up on the Internet. Do you want to see the website?"

"No, I don't."

He was arranging some of the items on the tables and it was almost as if this wasn't even worth discussing, but I kept on bugging him anyway. "Grey Wolf, if you were me, what would you do?"

"I already gave you the answer. I wouldn't go. It's too cold."

"So you don't think I should go then, right?"

"Here's my answer. If it were me I wouldn't go, but it's not my decision, it's yours. You're the one who is going to have to decide. You have to do what's right for you. Just give it some serious thought. It gets very, very cold up there and it stays that way for months."

I listened intently and then I said, "You're right. I hate the cold. I don't know what I was thinking. I wouldn't last. I'll look for another job here in California and forget about Montana. Thanks, Grey Wolf."

I walked out of the store relieved. I did the right thing. I asked an Indian what I should do and even the Indian didn't think I should go. My mind was made up. I was not going to go to Montana.

I got in my car and drove over to Trader Joe's to pick up something for dinner and maybe a bottle of wine to help me relax. As I entered the parking lot, there it was — right in front of me — a huge Mack truck. While I don't remember the company logo, right underneath it were the words: "BILLINGS MONTANA".

No! No! This can't be happening to me. I felt like I was in an episode of *Twilight Zone*. I sat there and stared at the truck hoping it was a hallucination. But it wasn't a hallucination, it was reality that stared back at me.

I couldn't move my car because that big Mack truck was parked right in front of me. I was stuck. I moaned, "Oh, noooooooo." I realized then that if I didn't go to Montana, I would be stuck for the rest of my life never accomplishing anything because I failed to "embrace my destiny." My future was laid out before me as clear as day, but I didn't want to embrace it. I felt like if I didn't go to

Montana something bad would happen to me, like Jonah in the Old Testament. God called him to Nineveh and when he refused the call he took sail in the opposite direction. As the boat set sail it encountered a terrible storm. In desperation, the crew drew lots and when it was determined that Jonah was the cause of the disastrous voyage they were on, they tossed him overboard. The storm ceased, but Jonah was swallowed up by a whale only to be spit out three days later. Jonah eventually answered the call to go to Nineveh. I felt that if I didn't go to Montana, I would end up in the belly of a whale. That was my choice — an Indian reservation in Montana or the belly of a whale. So now I knew what I was supposed to do, I just didn't want to do it.

CHAPTER FIVE

RING LAKE RANCH DID HAVE THE ANSWER

The next day, I finally answered the emails from the tiny little Indian school in Montana. After missing several dates for interviews, they were still interested in me. Either that or nobody else wanted the job. Faye was my contact and she never gave up. In my email I told her that I was interested in the position if it was still available. She emailed me the application and told me to fax it back to her as soon as possible.

I did all I could to overcome the resistance that welled up inside of me and sat down and forced myself to fill out the application. My job history for the past few years was pretty checkered and I thought for a moment that they might see it as a red flag and pass on me. I completed the application anyway and then I stopped at Dolores' office to ask her if I could use her fax machine.

"What are you faxing?"

"A job application."

"For what?"

"It's a little Indian school, up in Montana."

Dolores was dumbfounded. "Indian school? Montana? Why would you do that?"

"Because no one else wants me. I sent out resumes all over the country and this is the only school that responded. I'm not getting any other replies."

"This isn't a Catholic school, is it?"

"Yes, it is."

She couldn't believe I was applying for a job at another Catholic school, but she let me use her fax machine just the same. The fax went through and I left Dolores' office. I had only driven a few miles when my cell phone rang. I pulled over to the side of the road and answered the call. It was Faye. I don't even think it had been ten minutes from when I had faxed over the application. "Hi, Luella we are so happy to get your application. When can you come up for your interview?" I felt a gnawing in my stomach. This preposterous idea was becoming a reality.

I asked her if it was possible to do a phone interview, since that would save me the cost of a flight to Montana. She told me they required an in-person interview, so the teacher could see firsthand where they would be living. I asked if the school reimbursed travel expenses and they didn't. I went ahead and told her to email me a couple of dates and I would get back to her.

Once I got off the phone with Faye, I called Dolores.

"Dolores, you're not going to believe this, but they just called me for an interview. I just faxed my application a few minutes ago!"

"Boy, they must be really desperate."

"Thanks, Dolores," I said in despair.

That night I went to Dolores' house to use her computer. Mine was having some issues. She asked me what I was doing and I told her, "I'm booking a flight to Montana."

"You're not really serious about taking that job, are you? I thought that you were done with Catholic schools and now here you are going up to Montana to interview for another Catholic school?"

"Dolores, I'm not going to take that job. I'm just going up there so I can eliminate it and then come back to LA and get a job here."

"Then why bother going, if you're not going to take the job?"

"I just want to go up there and check it out."

"Check it out? Check out what? A job in the middle of nowhere in a state that has freezing cold temperatures half the year. Do I have to remind you that you hate the cold? You're from Massachusetts. Isn't that the reason why you moved out here in the first place, to get out of the cold? Remember that time we went to Vegas and you had the heater on in the middle of the summer?"

"Look, I'm just going to spend a few days on an Indian reservation and that's it. I'll fly into Billings, pick up a rental car, drive out to the Little Bighorn Battlefield, buy some souvenirs and then head out to the reservation. I'll stay there for a few days, have my interview and then come home. It will be like a retreat."

"Didn't you just go on a retreat?"

"So, I'll go on another one."

"They're paying for your flight, right?"

"No," I said sheepishly.

Dolores was in disbelief. "You mean, they're not even paying for your ticket? You have to pay for it yourself? I think you're spending a lot of money for nothing."

Dolores was right. My ticket cost a small fortune, but I put it on my credit card anyway.

There was a small part of me that thought this still wasn't going to happen. I saw it as some kind of "Abraham" test like when God called Abraham to sacrifice his son Isaac. Of course, Abraham didn't want to do it, but he was willing to do it. On the way up the mountain, Isaac kept asking, "Where's the sacrifice?" Once they got to the top of the mountain and Isaac realized that he was the sacrifice, a ram caught in the thicket suddenly appeared and Isaac was spared. I thought that if I was willing to go up to the reservation and interview for the job, it would convince God that I would make any sacrifice I was called to make, but that at the last hour, God would provide a job for me back in Los Angeles. 'It's just a test' I told myself. 'It's only a test.'

Once I got to Montana I realized that it wasn't a test.

Before leaving for the reservation, I decided to call Carl at the Ring Lake Ranch and let him know what I was up to. Maybe he would have some insight for me.

"Hey, Carl, it's Luella. Remember me?"

"Of course, I do. Did you find a job yet?"

"That's why I was calling you. Guess what, I'm going to be back up in your neck of the woods. I'm interviewing for a job up in Montana."

"You're kidding. Where?"

"A little Indian school."

"What's the name of the school?"

When I told him the name of the school, he started laughing. I got scared. What did he know that I didn't?

"What's so funny, Carl? Tell me. Do you know something about that school that I should know?"

"Remember Carole, the hike leader?"

"Yes."

"That's where she's working."

"You're kidding. Hey, wait a minute. Is she applying for the same job?"

I thought for a split second I might be off the hook because if she were applying for the same job I would do the Christian thing and back out and let her have it.

"No, it's not the same job. She was hired in May, so I know for sure it's not the same job."

"So, if I get this job, I will already know somebody up there?"

"Yes! Yes! You already have a friend in Montana!"

It seemed like a coincidence, but it was just one more "sign" that I was meant to go to Montana. So, I did find the answer I was looking for at the Ring Lake Ranch after all.

CHAPTER SIX

IS HEAT INCLUDED?

Wednesday, August 11, 2010 I flew from Los Angeles to Billings with a stop in Salt Lake City, Utah for a quick change of planes. The date of my flight, the exact flight, the plane change in Salt Lake City, and my seat assignment was not at all a random set of circumstances.

I ended up sitting next to a soft-spoken, incredibly intelligent woman named Adele. We talked as though we had known each other for a lifetime and maybe we had. Usually, I try to avoid talking to the person I'm sitting next to on a flight and they do the same. I'm always relieved when the person next to me takes out a book before the plane even takes off. When I'm not so lucky and the person next to me wants to strike up a conversation, I've been known to say, "Me, no speak English" or "Me English no too good." This doesn't always work though. I tried it once on a flight from Florida to Rio, Brazil. When the guy next to me wanted to chat, I said, "Me English no good." Then once the flight took off and the attendant came around with the drink cart, I said in very good English, "I'll have a Coke." Then I felt like a jerk when the guy looked at me and said, "Your English sounds pretty good to me."

But now on this flight up to Billings, the conversation with Adele seemed to flow effortlessly. Adele was smart. She was a writer. She was an intellectual. We had a lively and engaging conversation the entire flight. Adele had roots in Montana, but had lived in Los Angeles for quite some time. When she asked me why I was going to Montana, I told her it was just for a visit. We parted ways when the flight landed, but not before we exchanged our contact information. And I am so glad I did. I did not realize at the time how serendipitous our encounter was. Adele became a lifelong friend and confidante and all because I had the good fortune of sitting next to her on a plane to Montana to interview for a job that I didn't even want.

Once off the plane, I claimed my baggage and then made my way to the car rental desk, rented a car, and headed to the reservation. On the way, I made one stop at the Little Bighorn Battlefield just as I had planned. I visited the museum and the site of Custer's grave before they transported his body back to West Point. I listened to the talk given by the ranger, who I later found out was a teacher at my soon-to-be place of employment.

It had been a long day. I had been up since 4:00 a.m., driven to the airport, flown from Los Angeles to Utah, changed planes in Salt Lake City, landed in Billings, and then driven to the Little Bighorn Battlefield. I was exhausted, but I still had another forty-five-minute drive ahead of me.

Finally, I arrived. It was around 7:00 p.m. when I pulled into the parking lot. I stopped at the sight. This was it? It was nothing like what I had expected. All along, I had pictured some god-forsaken property with a couple of dilapidated trailers for classrooms, a run-down administration building, and a neglected playground. But it was nothing like that. The campus was absolutely gorgeous, more reminiscent of a community college campus than any high school campus I had ever been on. A series of modern buildings that housed the classrooms sprawled across the wide-open space. Rows of uneven, yet perfectly arranged hills surrounded the entire campus.

To add to the beauty of it all, the weather was heavenly; the temperature was perfect. The air was dry, not too hot, a bit of a breeze. There was a sense of peace and calm that I had not felt in quite a long time. Maybe it was the big sky or the surrounding hills; whatever it was, there was something very special going on here. As I stood in awe I wondered what could have brought me to this place. What force could have placed all the signs and coincidences that led me here? It was one of those moments when I was so glad that I hadn't listened to what everyone else had told me. I would have missed out on something truly magical and mystical. It's one thing when you get to a really special place that you have been anticipating. It is quite another when you get to a special place that you had no idea was there waiting for you.

The campus was deserted. It was early August, no students or faculty, but I did see a priest on the grounds. He was walking over to his Jeep, so I hurried over to him and introduced myself, "Hi, I'm Luella. I have an interview tomorrow. I am supposed to stay at the friary tonight. Can you tell me where that is?"

He was an elderly man, but very agile. He was Father Paschal, the priest for the school and several other parishes in the area.

"Oh, we are happy to have you here. Follow me and I will show you were the friary is."

Only a short distance from the parking lot, he walked me to the entrance of the friary and introduced me to the campus security guard who showed me to my room for the next two nights. Once I unpacked my things I took full advantage of the long stretch of daylight and went out to canvas the school grounds.

I was all alone as I walked the entire campus, but I didn't feel scared at all. I felt as though I had the whole place to myself. The grounds were expansive, dotted with a series of buildings, playgrounds, and basketball courts all arranged as though nature's hills and trees created a special niche for the school to dwell in. There was a gymnasium, a chapel, and even a museum. All were closed. There wasn't a soul in sight. I loved it that I could snoop around without anyone asking me if I needed any help. I was able to peer into a few of the classrooms. They were all modern and well equipped with neatly arranged desks and plenty of room for activities. This wasn't so bad after all.

But this was Montana. It wasn't California. It was beautiful. Big Sky. Rolling Hills. Magnificent Sunsets. But was it me? Could I live here? In the middle of nowhere? Could I pack up and move here with my three cats? How would I even do that? Where would I live? Or even more importantly, could I survive a Montana winter?

There was still more for me to see. As I walked across the campus and behind the chapel, I stumbled upon an open area dotted with large, towering cottonwood trees. Right smack in the middle sat an irresistible swing set. I rushed over, took a seat and started to swing as high as I could. Every time I swung upward, my stomach fluttered. I had a real, genuine happy feeling inside of me, just like when I was a little kid. A woman approached out of nowhere. She scared me at first, but she didn't seem to be threatened by me at all. And then she commented, "Isn't the weather beautiful!"

"Yes, it is beautiful here," I remarked back. I couldn't believe I said that, but it was true. The evening was beautiful.

I don't know how long I stayed out there. I had lost complete track of time, but I eventually made my way back to the friary. I was the only one staying there so I had the entire floor to myself except for the Indian pictures that hung on the halls.

Before I went to sleep I looked out the window at the most beautiful starlit sky. I was so glad I had made the trip. My feelings of hesitation and anxiety about coming up here were gone, at least for the moment, and I started to really want this job.

I woke up bright and early the next morning and headed to the main administration building. I introduced myself to the receptionist and told her I had an interview with Sister Bernadette, the Mission Director. The receptionist told me that Sister Bernadette was in a meeting and suggested that I visit the school's museum and when Sister Bernadette was finished with her meeting she would send her over to me.

The museum, while small, offered an authentic display of Native American artifacts, documents, clothing, and beadwork of the Northern Cheyenne people. And of course, it had a gift shop. I was only there a short time when Sister Bernadette entered the museum, approached me with a big smile and a warm handshake, and escorted me to her office.

Once in her office, she introduced me to the human resources director and after a few pleasantries, so began the process. Sister Bernadette conducted a very professional interview. She asked me a series of questions about my philosophy of education, what discipline procedures I used, and examples of creative techniques that worked well for me in the classroom.

Sister Bernadette asked me if I had any questions.

"Yes," I said. "Where would I be living?"

"Here in the village. We have housing right here in the village, a short walk from the school."

"And I would have my own place?"

"Yes. You would have your own house."

"Really? I would have my own house? I wouldn't have to share with anyone?"

"No, you wouldn't have to share with anyone. It would be your house."

I had never had my own house. This was looking pretty good. I was thinking it was going to be some sort of dorm-style existence sharing the kitchen, bathroom and living room with other teachers and I just couldn't handle that, not at my age. My next burning question, no pun intended, was, "What about heat? Do the houses have heat?"

She looked at me with a smile, "Oh yes, the houses have heat."

"You're sure?"

She nodded, "Yes, I'm sure. It's included in your rent."

"Really, heat is included? I don't have to pay for it?"

"No, you don't have to pay for it. It's included in your rent."

"You're sure."

"Yes, I'm sure."

"Can I see the houses?"

"Yes, of course. John Walks Along, he's in charge of housing. He can show you the houses that are available."

At first I thought she meant when John walks along or when John comes by he could show me the houses, but John Walks Along was his name.

He came by, picked me up in his truck, and we headed over to the village, just about a mile from the school. He pointed out the few houses that were still left. It was August and most of the houses were taken by other teachers who had already been hired. Then I saw it, a brightly colored yellow house on the corner of a cul-de-sac with a big cottonwood tree in the front yard. "Is that one still available?" I asked.

He nodded his head yes.

"Can I see it?"

He nodded his head again.

I picked that house for one reason. It was yellow. I thought yellow was a happy color and if I ever got depressed, at least when I came home I would have a yellow house to cheer me up.

He pulled in the driveway and we went inside. The house was small, but it had a cozy living room space, a place for a small dining room table, a kitchen, a bathroom, and three bedrooms. 'One for each one of my cats,' I thought. All the rooms had been freshly painted and they were in the process of installing new carpeting. I walked up and down the hall several times. "This might work. This might actually work," I murmured to myself. I would have my own house and I could walk to school, but most importantly, I could provide a nice home for my cats.

"How much?" I asked.

He hesitated, "Well, this one has three bedrooms so it's going to cost you a little more."

I cringed. "How much?"

"This house rents for $342.00. We usually deduct it out of your pay check."

"$342.00?" I was in disbelief.

He nodded his head. While I've never made a lot of money, I have come across some good deals in my life and this was one of them. $342.00 for a three bedroom on a cul-de-sac? That was a deal! I could actually see myself living here.

"What about heat? Is there heat?"

He nodded his head yes and pointed to the floor heaters that ran along the base of the walls. Each room had its own floor heater.

"And they work, right?"

He nodded his head.

"And it's included in the $342.00 right?"

He nodded again.

"You're sure."

He nodded again and then gave me that look. You know…that look they give you when you are starting to get on someone's nerves, but I had to be sure that there was heat. I said, "I'll take it."

He told me they would have the carpeting done by the time I moved in. We got in the truck and headed back to school and then came the moment of truth.

"Do you have pets?"

I hesitated. "Yes. I have cats."

"We have a two pet maximum."

I thought, 'Well, that's it. That's the reason not to take the job. Just tell him, "Oh no, what a shame. I have three cats. I guess I can't take the job." Just say it. Say it. Tell him that you have three cats.'

I looked at him and said, "Yeah, that's okay. I have two."

"We charge $20.00 a month rent for each cat."

"I'm okay with that." That was it. It was a done deal. I was moving to Montana with my three cats. Moo Moo would be my stowaway.

It was still morning and I had the rest of the day to check out the area. I drove into town and through it in about two minutes. There were two trading posts, a little store for movie rentals, two diners, a post office, and a bank. Down the road was a gas station and another little trading post. The population was 400. There were more people living in my condominium complex in Los Angeles.

With a whole day in front of me, I headed to Colstrip where I had once considered living. It was forty-five miles from the school, a nice two-lane drive with no traffic. Once I got to Colstrip, I grabbed a bite to eat and then headed back. I still had the whole afternoon, so I headed in the opposite direction to another little tiny town called Broadus. It had a few more options; a saloon, a motel, a few grocery stores, antique shop, a tire store, and a corral for rodeos. I was in a different part of the world for sure. I headed back to the friary and got a good night's sleep before going back to Los Angeles.

The next morning as I was leaving the friary, I ran into the custodian. He asked me how I liked the school. I said, "Very much so."

Then as he passed by, he casually mentioned, "You're the second person to interview for the job. Another person interviewed last week."

I was stunned. I thought I was the one for the job!

"What? What?" I said to God under my breath. "Somebody else interviewed for this job? I thought this was my job. What's with the Ring Lake Ranch and all the Montana signs? And the Indian pointing me in the right direction. Now that I want the job, you're going to give it to somebody else? Fine, then. I didn't want this job to begin with." That's what I told God.

I made my way down to the parking lot and as I was getting into my car, I saw Sister Bernadette waving to me from her office. I went towards the building as she came out to greet me. "We will be checking your references and you should be expecting a call from us early next week. School starts in ten days." It wasn't official, but I felt I had the job. "Thank you, Sister, I'll wait for your call."

I drove to the airport, dropped off the car, and boarded my flight home. Okay, so now I was pretty sure I had the job and everything felt right. Then I had a two-hour layover in Salt Lake City and as I sat in the airport, it suddenly hit me. I started to panic, 'I can't do this. I really can't do this.' The thought of leaving Southern California and moving to Montana brought me overwhelming anxiety. I was relieved that I had a job, but then another part of me dreaded all that it would entail. It was like being at the end of a diving board and knowing that I had to jump, but I didn't have the courage to do it.

I decided to call my friend Evy. I don't know why out of all my friends I decided to call her, but she was the right one to call. She was so excited for me, even a bit envious.

"This will be wonderful for you. It will be good for you to get out of Los Angeles and spend some time in Montana. I wish I could go live in Montana."

"Really?"

"Yes, I would love to go to Montana — to get away from the city and enjoy the wide open space, the beautiful scenery. I'm envious!"

"But what about my cats?" Evy was a cat person, just like me.

"Your cats will be fine. They will love it up there. Even cats need a change of scenery."

"Do you think they'll be able to make the move?"

"Yes, I had a friend who traveled from California to New Jersey with her cat in the car. They'll be fine."

I felt a lot better after talking to Evy.

Then I called my friends George and Edie, a beautiful couple I had known for years. They were like second parents to me. Few people are ever so fortunate to have a second set of parents, but for me, my parents in heaven sent me George and Edie for times like these. When I told Edie about my plans to move to Montana, she too was very excited for me and she even said, "I think you might meet a man up there." That made me laugh! They called my flight and I boarded the plane back to Los Angeles.

That weekend I waited with anticipation. The human resources director called me on Monday, August 16th and left a message offering me the position. I slept on it and called them back the next day and accepted it. That was August 17th, school started on the 26th.

CHAPTER SEVEN

U-HAUL MY ASS

The past few months had been incredibly stressful. You would think that finding a job would give me a little bit of relief, yet the opposite was true. I don't know which is worse, the anxiety over losing a job or finding a job that requires you to move fifteen hundred miles in less than ten days. I sat at my desk and struggled to come up with a way for me and my three cats to get back up to the reservation. To complicate matters I had the most intense, pounding headache that seemed to dig into my brain with every passing moment.

I thought about my condo. Should I rent it out? Who would I rent it out to? How would I advertise? If I rented out my condo, I would have to move all my stuff out. I didn't plan on taking all my stuff to Montana, so I would have to put what I didn't take to Montana into storage. If someone was interested in renting, then I would have to check references. What if they didn't pay the rent or even worse, what if they destroyed my condo? This relentless ping pong game going on in my head continued for hours until I finally came to the obvious conclusion that renting my condo would just create more problems. Besides, I knew with my salary I could pay my rent in Montana and my mortgage in Los Angeles. Not only that, but if I only lasted a few months in Montana, which was a strong possibility, I would have a place to come home to. So I decided not to rent out my condo.

I still had to figure out how was I going to get back to Montana. I analyzed each and every possible scenario. I could pack everything into my car and drive up, but my car already had 200,000 miles on it and I wasn't sure if it could even go the distance. What if my car broke down in the middle of nowhere and I had to wait hours for AAA to show up and the only repair shop was miles away and then what if it took days to repair and I got to school late? No, that wasn't an option. Plus, I didn't really need a car. Once I got to

Montana, I could walk to school. If I needed a ride, I was sure someone from school or the village could help me out.

The idea of a motorhome popped into my head. Yeah, I could do that. I could pack all my things in a motorhome, drive up to Montana and not worry about staying in a hotel along the way. That seemed like a really good idea until I called up a couple of motorhome rental places and got their quotes. Definitely out of my price range. So that option was out. Next, I thought about renting a car and pulling a small U-Haul trailer behind me. I could pack a few things, but if I did that I would have to buy furniture once I got to Montana. How would I get to a furniture store in Billings if I didn't have a car? Not only that, but how would I get the rental car back to Los Angeles? Then it dawned on me, what about a U-Haul truck? That made more sense than a trailer. That was the answer to my dilemma. There was a U-Haul dealer a few miles from where I lived. I passed by it all the time. I called them up and ran through my list of questions.

"How much is a U-Haul?"

"Depends on the size."

"What are the sizes?"

"10, 15, 20, or 26-foot."

The 10-foot was obviously the cheapest, so that was my choice.

"Do you have a 10-foot available?"

"Yes."

"Can I bring my animals with me?"

"Yes."

"Can I put it on my credit card?"

"Yes."

"I want to go to Montana. Is there a place that I can drop it off?"

"Yes, we have locations in Montana. The best place would be for you to drop it off at the airport in Billings."

Once I figured out how I was going to get to Montana that agonizing headache began to disappear. But there was another problem. While driving up to Montana in a U-Haul seemed like the most practical choice, I knew in a million years, I could never do this on my own. I needed Dolores.

She thought I was crazy for going on the interview. Now she was really going to think I was crazy. I didn't know how I was going to ask her to drive me and my three cats to Montana. I mean, how do you ask someone to drive you fifteen hundred miles in a U-Haul? I decided to let the conversation unfold spontaneously.

I went down to her place and knocked on the door. As soon as she opened the door and invited me in, her first question was, "So, did you eliminate it?"

I hesitated to tell her, but then I blurted it out, "No, I'm actually going to take the job."

"What? You're going to take that job? I thought you were going up there to eliminate it?"

"Yeah, I thought I was going to do that too, but it didn't turn out the way I thought."

"So, you're really going to Montana?"

"Yeah, I am."

"Are you sure about this? I mean, you really want to go to Montana?" She wasn't sold on this whole Montana idea.

Then she asked, "What are you going to teach?

I hesitated, and then I admitted it, "Religion."

"Religion! Let me get this straight. You are going to move to an Indian reservation in Montana so you can teach religion at another Catholic school? After all they did to you! They fired you! Why would you even think of teaching at another Catholic school?"

"I don't really have a choice, Dolores. I need a job and this is the only school that wants me."

"Do you have a place to live?"

"Yeah, I have a three-bedroom house on a cul-de-sac. Right there on the reservation. I can walk to school." I wanted to put a really good spin on it.

"What about your cats?"

She knew how I felt about my cats.

"I'm going to take them with me."

"Have you figured out how you are going to get up there?"

"Yeah, I have. I'm going to rent a U-Haul." My voice got a little shaky.

"You, drive a U-Haul up to Montana?" Dolores said with just a tiny hint of sarcasm.

"Yeah, that's what I wanted to talk to you about."

"Oh, no! If you think I'm going to drive you and your three cats up to Montana in a U-Haul so you can teach on an Indian reservation, think again."

"Oh, c'mon, Dolores, think how much fun it's going to be. You, me, driving a U-Haul to Montana with my three cats. You've never been to Montana. You get to see that big sky that everyone is always talking about. And you get to breathe in the fresh air of Montana. C'mon, Dolores, don't you want to go to Montana?"

"No, I don't." She was being honest. Who in their right mind would want to drive me and my three cats up to Montana in a U-Haul?

"Oh, Dolores, think about it. Things like this only happen once in a lifetime. It's a great opportunity for the both of us to see another part of the country. And you get to go to an Indian reservation too."

"Luella, are you sure? Are you sure you really want to leave California and go live and teach on an Indian reservation?"

"I don't have a choice, Dolores. No one else wants me."

"I'm sorry Luella, but I can't drive you up to Montana. Besides, it's really busy at work and I don't think I can get the time off anyway." That was her final word. I distinctly remember leaving her house and as I closed the door behind me I felt a sense of relief. I guess I wasn't going to Montana after all because there was no way I could drive a U-Haul up to the reservation all by myself.

Dolores called me the next day. "Alright, Luella, I pulled it up on the internet. We drive through Nevada, a little bit of Arizona, then Utah, then Wyoming, and then we get to Montana."

"You'll do that for me? You'll really do that for me?"

"Yeah, I'll do it for you. I already requested the time off."

I was going to Montana after all! Dolores came with me to pick up the U-Haul. At this stage everything became mechanical. It was the only way I could slap almost $2000.00 on my credit card for a U-Haul rental. That had to have been the biggest credit card purchase I had ever made in my life. It left me with a big knot in my stomach, but at least my headache had gone away.

The next few days were a blur. I didn't have time to contact all my friends to let them know I was leaving California. I figured I could call them in the U-Haul on the way up, but I did want to talk to my dear friend Eufemia before I left. Even though I had not known her for very long, I considered her to be a very good friend. She was Filipino, tiny in size, never quite reaching five feet, but a great big heart. She was a nursing instructor at UCLA and her profession fit her perfectly. She was one of the most caring and giving persons to ever cross my path.

It was after midnight when I sent her an email telling her I was leaving for Montana in two days. I was so happy when she emailed me back right away. We met for coffee the next morning and I gave her the abbreviated version of what had happened. She asked me what I was taking with me. When I told her I wasn't taking that much since I didn't have that much to begin with, she told me she would come back that night with some essentials. I told her she didn't have to, but she insisted.

That night Eufemia brought me two wool turquoise-colored blankets, two brand new Eddie Bauer hooded ski jackets, a couple sets of towels, two cotton bathrobes, and two blow-up beds. Her generosity was overwhelming and it made the move a lot easier, but I was still very apprehensive about what I was getting myself into.

The next day was surreal. It was still hard for me to believe that I was moving to Montana to live and teach on an Indian reservation. I don't think I will ever forget that day or that feeling, or rather lack of feeling. I was just going through the motions of packing up the U-Haul. If I thought about what I was doing, I would have lost the courage to begin the journey, so I just didn't think about it. I had made big moves before. I moved from Massachusetts to California, California to Brazil, Brazil to American Samoa, but those were all moves that I intended on making and they happened over time. This move was different. It was sudden and I never envisioned living on an Indian reservation in Montana at this stage in my life.

But I knew that if I didn't do this my life would stall and I would never accomplish anything grand because I didn't "embrace my destiny" and do what I was supposed to in Montana. My life would be ordinary, mediocre, not worth living. I didn't want that, so I just kept packing up the U-Haul. The maintenance worker in my building was kind enough to help me load up the heavy stuff and Dolores helped me load up the small stuff.

I was most worried about my cats. I didn't want anything to happen to them. They were confused seeing all the stuff being taken out of our condo. They didn't know what was happening and then it was time for them to get in their kennels and take their places in between Dolores and me. I stacked them one on top of each other. Moo Moo, appropriately named for her black and white cow spots, was my youngest and I thought she could take the ride easier than the others, so she was on the bottom. Tiger, my ginger cat, had a very sensitive stomach so he was stacked in the middle, and Juanita, my littlest one was on the top. She was a tortoise shell cat. And then we were off.

We had a lot of time in the U-Haul; time to talk and time for me to brood over the injustice I had fallen victim to.

"I'm still pissed off at that priest who got me fired."

"He's just a pawn."

"What do you mean, he's just a pawn?"

"He's a pawn. God is using him to get you to come up to this reservation and do whatever it is you're supposed to do up here. Look at all the things you've done as a teacher. You started out in Los Angeles and then you went to Brazil and you taught there and then you went to Samoa and look at what you did there. Didn't your students win some award?"

"Yeah, they got first place in a singing competition."

"See… who knows what you'll do up here."

"Yeah, I know, but I'm still pissed off."

I convinced myself that Dolores was right. That priest was just a pawn. Obviously this was the only way for me to go to Montana because I never would have come up with this idea on my own. I was glad that Dolores was driving me up there. It wasn't just a ride that I needed, I needed the moral and emotional support too.

That first night we got as far as St. George, Utah. When I checked in at the front desk, I got two rooms, one for me and one for Dolores. Dolores wasn't really a cat person, plus I wanted her to have a little time for herself on the trip. At the desk, I didn't tell them I had three cats. I was just going to sneak them in. But once I went out to the U-Haul to get my cats, I realized that there were cameras all over the property and I knew I couldn't get them in without being caught.

I went back to the front desk and sheepishly confessed, "Oh, I forgot to mention that I have three cats with me." I didn't know how she was going to react, but I think she must have been an animal lover too because she completely understood.

"Oh, no problem! We have special rooms available for pets."

I was relieved. It was already late and I couldn't imagine getting back into the U-Haul and trying to find a pet-friendly hotel, especially after Dolores had been driving for ten hours. The clerk at the front desk quickly changed my room to a pet-friendly one and she gave Dolores a room right next to me and my cats.

Getting my cats from the U-Haul into the hotel room required coordination, stamina, and patience. Dolores waited in the U-Haul, while I brought Juanita in first, left her in the hotel room, in her kennel. Then I went back to the U-Haul to get Tiger and brought him into the hotel room, and then I went out again and grabbed Moo Moo and brought her into the hotel.

Once all my cats were safe and sound, Dolores and I brought our baggage up to our rooms. My cats slept in their kennels, but I placed them on the bed so they could see me and each other. I never took them out of their kennels, except to clean it out. I met with their vet before we left to get his advice on traveling with three cats in a U-Haul up to Montana. He was confident that they could make the trip, but he made it quite clear, "Don't take them out of their kennels, no matter what. They are not like dogs. No matter what, keep them in their kennels."

The next day, leaving the hotel, we packed up the cats in reverse. Dolores waited in the U-Haul as I brought Moo Moo out and placed her first in between the two seats. Then I went back to get Tiger and placed his kennel on top of Moo Moo's. Then I got Juanita and placed her kennel on top of Tiger's. I repeated this procedure every night and every morning for three days until we got to the reservation. A lot of people have asked me how I got my cats up to Montana in a U-Haul, and that's how I did it.

Back on the highway Dolores was driving really fast. It was making me nervous. "Dolores can you please slow down?"

She would slow down for a few minutes and then pick up speed. Maybe she wasn't aware of how fast she was going, but it really bothered me. "Dolores, you want me to drive?"

"No, I'm okay. You just take care of your cats. I'm fine with driving."

We had been on the road for a few hours when all of a sudden the highway turned into a main street and then out of nowhere a flashing blue light was right behind us.

"I knew it. I knew this was going to happen. How many times did I say, 'Dolores, will you please slow down?'"

Dolores said nothing as she pulled the U-Haul over to the side of the road.

"Dolores, do you want me to do the talking?"

"No, I don't. I'll handle this one." She was a little bit irritated.

"Are you sure you don't want me to talk?"

"Yes, I'm sure."

The cop approached Dolores' side of the U-Haul and with that authoritative tone, said, "Ma'am can I see your driver's license?"

Dolores gave him her license, paused and said woefully, "You're not going to give me a ticket are you?"

It was a speed trap for sure. All of a sudden the highway turned into a town and the speed limit changed in a blink of an eye.

The officer took out his pad and pen.

"Oh, c'mon, you're not going to give me a ticket, are you? I'm driving my friend up to Montana. She's going to be teaching on an Indian reservation."

He didn't even respond and just as he was about to start writing, Dolores gave it another try. "Oh, c'mon she's a teacher! She's going to work on an Indian reservation. I'm giving her a ride up there."

He wrote out the ticket anyway.

I started to get out of the U-Haul and that got him angry. He yelled over at me, "Where are you going?"

I said very politely, "I need to go to the bathroom. Can I do that?" Once he gave me permission I walked across the street to a convenience store to take a pee and pick up a couple of sodas. By the time I got back to the U-Haul, the police officer had left and Dolores was sitting there with the ticket in her hand. "I'm so sorry Dolores. I really am. I'll pay you as soon as I get my first paycheck."

But it wasn't as bad as I thought. The officer did show some mercy and wrote out the ticket for a reduced speed. I guess Dolores made him feel guilty enough to show a little leniency for driving a teacher up to an Indian reservation to teach. We got back on the road, but this time a little slower. Even with the unexpected stop by the cop, by nightfall we made it as far as Rock Springs, Wyoming. We went through the nightly ritual of checking into a pet-friendly hotel and bringing the cats in one by one.

The next day, we left Rock Springs for the final leg of the journey. I again offered to do some of the driving, but Dolores was fine driving the rest of the way, in spite of getting a ticket. My original intention was to help out with some of the driving, but I think Dolores knew from the beginning that she'd be doing it all.

We were about midway through Wyoming when Dolores asked, "Is there anyone there who can help us unload the U-Haul?"

"Yeah, they told me that if we got to the village by 5:00 p.m., someone would be at the house to help us unload, but I don't want anyone to help us."

Dolores looked at me puzzled, "Why not?"

"Because I just don't want anyone to help us unload."

"Why not? I've been driving for three days and I really don't want to have to unload this when I get there."

"I just don't want anyone else to help us unload."

"Why not?"

So I had to confess. "Dolores, I don't want anyone to know that I have three cats. I am only allowed two and I could never leave one of them behind."

"Oh, alright, now I understand."

We made one last pit stop. We stopped in Sheridan, Wyoming to fill up on gas and get a few snacks. I knew that there were only two small grocery stores in the village, so I needed to stock up on some food for the next few days. When I came out of the supermarket, I looked up at the sky and saw the most beautiful rainbow etched across the horizon. I took it as another "sign." I felt like Noah. He had an ark for his animals and I had a U-Haul for mine and they both kept us safe.

We were almost there, but not quite. Dolores still had a bit more to go, a little under two hours. No more freeways or interstate highways, the last leg of the journey was a narrow two lane, long and winding road that led us deeper and deeper into the back country until we finally passed the sign that read "ENTERING THE NORTHERN CHEYENNE RESERVATION." After three days of driving we were finally there — on the reservation. Both of us got really quiet.

A few miles down the deserted road a small green and white sign announced that we had finally reached our destination. I pointed Dolores in the right direction through the village till we turned the corner to the little yellow house on the cul-de-sac.

"There it is. That's my house."

Dolores groaned, "Oh, no."

"Dolores, don't say that! It's really cute on the inside and it has everything I need."

We pulled into the driveway. It was about 10:00 p.m. The keys were left under the mat. No one would see me bringing in my three cats. We brought in a few things from the U-Haul — the blow-up beds from Eufemia, the grocery shopping we did in Sheridan and a change of clothes. Saturday we spent most of the day unloading the U-Haul, but later in the day, Dolores and I went for a walk around the campus. It was a beautiful day. The sun was shining, the sky was clear, and the temperature was perfect, but I was miserable. Dolores told me to "be happy."

"Easy for you to say, you're going back to California. I'm staying here."

"Luella, be happy. You have a job, a house. It's beautiful up here."

She was right. It was a beautiful day, just as beautiful as the very first day I had arrived on the reservation for my interview, but now things were different. I wasn't here for just a few days. No, I would be living here, so far away from my friends and what I had known in California. I was feeling homesick already and I had only been on the reservation for 24 hours. How would I last a year?

The next morning when Dolores was about to leave, she put her arms around me and gave me one last hug. That was when I broke down and started to cry like a baby. I mean really cry, like when your shoulders shake up and down uncontrollably. That's how I cried. Dolores was my last connection to California and I didn't want to let her go. I watched her as she walked out to the U-Haul. She looked back at me and waved, "Bye, Luella, bye." And then she got in the U-Haul and drove away.

CHAPTER EIGHT

MY FIRST POWWOW

And there I was in my little yellow house with my three cats. My tears stopped. The reality set in as I looked around at all the unpacking I still needed to do. I emptied all the boxes, hung up my clothes in the bedroom closet and arranged a few things in my kitchen.

The first thing I noticed about the reservation was the silence. In Los Angeles, I lived right by the freeway, so there was always a steady stream of traffic. Now the sound of a car passing by was only a remote possibility. I sat down on my couch and took a moment to pause and take in what had just happened to me over the past few months. It was astounding. I thought, 'I am on an Indian reservation. What an incredible experience lies before me, so why am I so sad? I shouldn't feel this way. I should be filled with joy and anticipation.' I couldn't figure out my emotions. When I first came to the reservation for my interview I felt a sense of peace and calm. Now I didn't feel any peace at all. Was this one of God's tricks, I wondered. Luring me to the reservation by giving me a false sense of serenity and security and now that I am here all I feel is discontent. I was so confused. All I could do was trust and accept that something really good was going to come from all of this in spite of how I felt.

The next day, Monday, I headed off to school for my first day teaching on an Indian reservation. School started on the previous Thursday, but since I was hired late and I was coming from Los Angeles, they cut me some slack. When I got to the campus the place was deserted, like in the summer. It was still early, about 7:30 a.m. There were no students, but I thought I would see at least a couple of teachers. I even wondered if school was in session yet. Did I get the dates wrong? Having no idea where my classroom was, I walked over to what I thought was the main building for the high school. When I went to open the door, it was locked, but a man saw me and quickly came over to the door and unlocked it for me. He introduced himself as the principal and I introduced myself as the teacher from Los Angeles. He was out of town for my interview, so this was the first impression for both of us. He grabbed some keys and seemed eager to show me where my classroom was. We had a pleasant conversation as we walked across the campus. When we got to my classroom, he unlocked and opened the door for me and wished me good luck in the new school year. I remember thinking, 'He seems like a pretty nice guy.' I was really looking forward to working with him. I guess you could say I was a bit overly optimistic.

My classroom was big and that was a good thing. It gave me a lot of room to work, room to move around, room to create, room to decorate, and room to grow. It was painted light blue. A row of closets filled with books, old poster boards, and a few classroom supplies lined one of the walls. There were tiny windows above the closets, too high up to see out of, but enough to let in a sliver of light. There was no view. I had a SMART Board. There were no desks, just long tables with two or three chairs at each table. There was a teacher's desk in the corner. As I began to arrange some of the items on my desk I heard the first announcement of the day come over the PA. It isn't unusual for students to be called over the PA, but it was their last names that took me by surprise — Lone Bear, Bull Coming, Shoulder Blade, Old Elk. I stopped dead in my tracks and thought, 'Oh my God, I really am on an Indian reservation!' This would be my 19th year teaching and I knew then it would be like no other.

A few minutes later the kids rolled in and I took the attendance. Then I introduced myself to the class. I told them where I was from, what universities I had graduated from, and what high schools I had taught at over the years. A student sitting in the back of the room called out, "Why did you come here?" His tone was more of a suspicious nature than genuine concern.

I answered truthfully, "Well, I lost my job and the unemployment rate in California is 12%." To which he replied, "Here on the reservation it's 50%."

Another student asked "How long do you think you will stay?" She seemed to be truly interested in me.

"Well, how long do most teachers stay?"

"Some leave at Thanksgiving or they go home for Christmas break and don't come back." That didn't sound too encouraging, but I was grateful for her honesty. I definitely had a challenge ahead of me.

"Well," I said, "I have a contract for a year and I intend on keeping it."

From the very beginning, I made every effort to connect with my students. The first few classes, I had them write bio poems. They wrote their first name at the top of their paper and then made a list of the things they loved, needed, gave, and wanted, and then their last name was included at the bottom. Again, I was intrigued with their last names.

The librarian later explained to me, the names were passed down from their great great great grandfathers who had gone on a vision quest and spent three or four days in the wilderness. After prayer and fasting, they would see a bear or an owl and that animal had a special message for them, so they took on the name of that animal. When they were forced onto the reservation and they were asked their names, they would say "Black Bear" or "Lone Bear" or "Little Owl." As generations followed, the names were passed down as last names.

I was also very conscientious about using the term Native American, but I noticed that they would say Indian. One day I asked the human resources director, "Is it Native American or is it Indian?" She said, "We're Indians, but if you want to say Native American, that's okay too." So I use the terms interchangeably.

They finished off their bio poems with pictures from magazines and their own personal artwork. Once they were done I had them read their bio poems to the class. This way, I got to know them, see their creativity and how well they related to each other. They enjoyed the activity, so I was off to a good start.

Later in the week, some of the students asked me if I was going to the powwow that weekend.

"What's a powwow?"

"You mean, you don't know what a powwow is?" They couldn't believe it!

While I had heard the term before, I didn't know much at all about them. Students were excited about explaining it to me.

"We all get together and dance!"

"There's lots of food!"

"And dance competitions."

"And there's always the drumbeat."

"Where is it?" I asked.

"It's right up the street," one student chimed in.

"You can walk there from here," said another.

"Okay, you convinced me. I'll see you at the powwow this weekend!"

Late Wednesday, I was walking home from school and guess who was walking directly towards me — Carole, the hike leader from the Ring Lake Ranch. Because of her schedule she started school a few days after I did. Boy, was I glad to see her! Even though I had only met her a few months before it was like seeing an old friend and it gave me a really good feeling. She had a big smile on her face and then we both cracked up laughing. I couldn't help but look back in amazement at the path that had been prepared for me. From the moment I got fired, everything from Sacajawea's gravesite, the Ring Lake Ranch, the "sign" on the freeway, the truck in Trader Joe's parking lot, everything seemed to lead me to this place in Montana. But there was still the big, "Why?" It would take me years to fully comprehend the meaning of all that was happening in my life.

That Friday, Carole and I ended up going to the powwow together. The 29th Annual Labor Day Powwow was a four-day event, Friday through Monday, held outdoors. Before we even got to the site, we could hear the drum. It permeated the entire grounds. It was the heartbeat of the powwow. The closer we got, the louder the drumbeat. Once we arrived, we looked out upon a big open lot with rows of benches arranged in a circle for spectators to observe the dancing and drumming that would take place in the center. Around the perimeter of the circle were various booths selling food, jewelry, and souvenirs. The biggest seller was the Indian taco. I had not heard of the Indian taco before. It was a lot like a Mexican taco with lettuce, tomato, and meat, but the outer shell was made with fry bread — a piece of dough deep-fried in oil. Being a vegetarian, I got the veggie taco.

After we got our tacos, Carole and I found a seat and watched the first dance of the night — the dance of the clowns. Native Americans came out dressed as clowns and competed for prize money by showing off their best dance moves. After the first dance, Carole and I circled the rim of the powwow and spotted a group of teachers sitting on the outer benches, so we went over to join them. We spent the next few hours watching an array of dancers and listening to various Native American songs while talking about the upcoming school year. The night ended, but not the powwow. That would continue throughout the entire weekend.

That night I walked home with Carole and another teacher, who I found out was from Anaheim, California. She was a friend of a student of mine who I had taught nearly 20 years ago. Suddenly I didn't feel so far away from home anymore.

The next day, Saturday, Carole invited me to go to Billings with her. Since I didn't have a car I took every chance I got whenever someone offered me a ride. It didn't matter if they were going to Billings or Sheridan I would always go along with them. Even though I had only been on the reservation for a week, I still wanted to use the opportunity to get a few items. Shopping in Montana was an entirely different experience. It was never a quick trip. It was more like transporting cargo. Since the reservation was so remote, an hour and a half to Sheridan, two hours to Billings, once you got to those cities you went to as many stores as possible and stocked up on as many items as could fit in the car before heading back.

On this trip we went to Granny's Attic, Cost Plus, Staples, and an organic food store, and our last stop was Target. I was so glad they had a Starbucks. While Carole did her shopping, I sat and I sipped my chai latte as I watched an unending line of customers come in and out of the store. For some reason, those familiar spots and things like a Starbucks chai latte seem to bring a little bit of comfort when you are far from home. With a two-hour drive ahead of us, we stopped for dinner at a Thai restaurant before we drove back.

The next day, Sunday, I went to church. I didn't really want to go. I was still a little bit mad at God, but I had to go to church because I was teaching in a Catholic school and I was supposed to be a practicing Catholic. The church was located on the school's campus, a short walk from where I lived. I had no excuse not to go. I couldn't say that I went to church in Lame Deer or Broadus because everyone knew I didn't have a car. The parish was really small and if I didn't show up for mass everyone would know, so, I had to go to church.

The church, which was more a chapel, was a blend of Native American spirituality and Catholic tradition. It was built in the shape of a tepee with a life size cross extending from the roof. The interior was a combination of Christian symbols — the crucifix and a statue of Mother Mary, as well as Native American symbols — the Medicine Wheel, cedar and sage bowls, and a picture of Blessed Kateri, who was later canonized in 2012. She was the first

Native American to become a saint in the Catholic Church. The Stations of the Cross, in the form of petroglyphs, were etched into the stone walls.

Father Paschal was the pastor. He was the first person I met when I pulled into the parking lot that day back in August when I came up for my interview. He was one of the kindest souls I had ever encountered. His face glowed like that of an angel and his voice was soft and soothing. He was a man of steadfast peace. His soul was at rest. I wished mine was. While Father Paschal's sermon that day was hopeful and encouraging, I still felt a lack of peace, an inner twisting and turning.

I thought that after being here for a week I would feel better, but my discontent seemed to deepen. I couldn't understand why. And then it started to sink in. I had been stripped of everything — my home, my friends, my students. I had no car, no TV. How was I going to make it through the next nine months? Why did I do this in the first place? I thought I was doing God's will, so why did I feel so empty inside? I was lost. I started to cry.

I did something that I hadn't done in years. I cracked the Bible. It was something Sister Louise taught us in the eighth grade. You ask God a question and next you crack open the Bible and blindly point to a passage and that's your answer. But you have to do it with faith and at this point in time, I had very little.

I first cracked the New Testament.

1 Corinthians 2:9 However, as it is written: "No eye has seen, no ear has heard, no mind has conceived what God has prepared for those who love him."

That's right. I never saw this coming. I skipped through some more pages.

Ephesians 2:10 For we are God's workmanship, created in Christ Jesus to do good works, which God prepared in advance for us to do.

Really? This is what You have been preparing me for?

Ephesians 3:20 Now to him who is able to do immeasurably more than all we ask or imagine, according to his power that is at work within us, to him be glory in the church and in Christ Jesus throughout all generations, for ever and ever! Amen.

This was definitely more than I could ever ask for or imagine, that's for sure. I flipped through some more pages.

Romans 8:18 I consider that our present sufferings are not worth comparing with the glory that will be revealed in us.

Okay, so something good is going to come out of this? Is that a promise?

These scripture verses, while positive, didn't offer me any consolation at all. If anything, I felt worse. They seemed to be such inspirational verses, yet I was still down in the dumps. I actually wrote down, "My sadness and tears creep in...where is joy in Montana? Where do I look for it?"

And then I decided to crack open the Old Testament.

Isaiah 33:2 O, Lord, be gracious to us; we long for you. Be our strength every morning, our salvation in time of distress.

Okay, I did feel some distress. And then a few passages further down...

Isaiah 33:6 He will be the sure foundation for your times, a rich store of salvation and wisdom and knowledge; the fear of the Lord is the key to this treasure.

Okay, I was getting close. Montana is known as the Treasure State, but this still didn't make any sense to me. I flipped through a few more pages.

Isaiah 35:3 Strengthen the feeble hands, steady the knees that give way; say to those with fearful hearts, "Be strong, do not fear; your God will come, he will come with vengeance, with divine retribution he will come to save you."

Okay, I liked the vengeance part because I was still pissed off at the priest who got me fired.

Isaiah 38:4-6 Then the word of the Lord came to Isaiah: "Go and tell Hezekiah, 'This is what the Lord, the God of your father David, says: I have heard your prayer and seen your tears; I will add fifteen years to your life. And I will deliver you and this city from the hand of the king of Assyria. I will defend this city.'"

Sometimes, I don't know if He really is hearing my prayer. And then I found it, the passages that fit my circumstances exactly.

Isaiah 38:13-14 I waited patiently till dawn, but like a lion he broke all my bones; day and night you made an end of me. I cried like a swift or thrush, I moaned like a mourning dove. My eyes grew weak as I looked to the heavens. I am troubled; O Lord, come to my aid! But what can I say? He has spoken to me, and he himself has done this. I will walk humbly all my years because of this anguish in my soul.

That last line kind of summed it up for me — anguish in my soul. Yep, that's exactly what I had — anguish in my soul.

I put down the Bible without having gained any consolation at all. I needed to do something positive so I decided to write down my goals for the next thirty-eight weeks, which at that time seemed like an eternity.

- Take good care of my cats

- Read Gandhi's autobiography (That 500-page Herculean task that sat on my coffee table for years without a page ever turning was finally going to be read.)

- Write twelve chapters of my book

- Keep a journal of my year on the Northern Cheyenne Reservation

- BE THE BEST LITTLE TEACHER I CAN BE (I actually wrote it all in caps.)

- Take a history class on the Northern Cheyenne People

- Go on as many trips as possible

- Learn about the culture

- Pray

- Have friendship

They weren't written in any particular order, but writing down my goals did make me feel a little bit better.

The next day was Labor Day and I stayed in my house and worked on my lesson plans for the week ahead. In the distance I could still hear the drumbeat of the powwow. It went on all morning and into the afternoon. Once I finished my lesson plans, I decided to go back to the powwow.

It was a beautiful day in Montana. The temperature was perfect; not too hot and not too cold. There were clear skies above me. It was a splendid, sunny afternoon. I ran into a few of my students and they looked fabulous dressed in their regalia. I was looking forward to seeing them dance.

It was perfect timing. I got there just as the grand entry had started. One of the chiefs said a prayer and then a line of military soldiers carrying the U.S. flag and their tribal nations' flags entered the ring. Following the military entrance there was a procession of spectacular Native dances. First came the men, then the women, and lastly the children. They formed a circle and continued to dance to the drumbeat for quite a long time. Later there were dances from different tribes and different age groups. I was quite intrigued with the "jingle" dance. The "jingle" sound came from the tops of tobacco cans that were curled and then sewn onto their regalia so that when they danced, they would "jingle," hence the name —

"jingle dance." I found out later that the jingle dance brings about healing. Fancy dance, gourd dance, and the grass dance were all a part of the powwow too.

I had traveled all over the world, totally oblivious to the magnificent cultural heritage that existed in my own country. I thought back to my meeting with Leonard months before when I wanted to go to Bhutan and he told me that I didn't have to go halfway around the world to have a life-changing experience. I could do that here in this country. He was right. He was right about another thing too. There are many beautiful places in the United States and Montana was one of them. Such words of wisdom — and from a tax accountant! The only thing is — I wanted a two-week transformational journey not a yearlong contract. That night when I went home I felt a little bit better, but I still didn't know why I was there.

CHAPTER NINE

NATIVE AMERICAN WEEK

The first two weeks of school passed without any major problems until I got my first paycheck. It wasn't the amount that shocked me, but stamped right on the front of my paycheck was: "Made possible through the generosity of our donors." Donors? What? What? I have to rely on donors for my pay? I went into a panic. What if nobody gives any money next month? That couldn't be right. Donors? Donors paid the salaries of all the teachers?

Then I asked one of the students how much tuition was and she looked at me bewildered and said, "What's that?" I asked another student and he didn't know what tuition was either.

When I explained what it was, they said, "No, we don't pay tuition."

"What? You don't pay tuition? Are you sure?"

"No, we don't pay tuition."

That can't be right. I had never worked at a school that was totally funded by donations, but it was true. The whole school ran on donations. As a matter of fact, this little tiny Indian school was actually one of the best run non-profit organizations in the country. Knowing that, I could breathe a little easier.

The school celebrated Native American Week September 22-24. The theme for the week was Honoring Our Elders: "Celebrating Those People Who Never Forgot." Monday and Tuesday the school was preparing for the event. On Wednesday and Thursday, regular classes were canceled and students and faculty had the opportunity to participate in a variety of workshops including Doll Making, Ladies' Cedar Bags, Bandolier for Gourd Dancing, Knife Sheaths, Gourds for Gourd Dancing, Hand Drums, Native Foods,

Ledger Art, Cheyenne Women's Seed Game, and Cheyenne Medicine Pouches.

I wanted to go to all of them, but I decided on "The Making of Medicine Pouches" with Charles Little Old Man and Marcelline Shoulder Blade as the presenters. It was a nice group, probably about fifteen. Most of them were my students, so I got to see them in a different light. The first thing Charles did was light a small bundle of sweet grass. Each one of us came forward and stood still as Charles waved the bundle around us while saying a special blessing. This was my very first smudging ceremony by a Native American.

After the smudging, we took our seats and Charles explained to us the significance of the medicine pouches. He told us that they are worn for protection and that medicine pouches were always given to men before a battle and that many of the American Indians currently fighting in Afghanistan wore medicine pouches around their necks.

We began by cutting a small piece of deerskin. For me that was really hard to do, being an animal lover and all, but I was trying to adapt to Native American ways. We folded the deerskin and sewed it into a pouch. As I stitched the sides of the medicine pouch together, I thought about who I wanted to give it to. I decided that I would give this medicine pouch to Dolores. Once the pouches were finished, we filled them with either sage or sweet grass. While most medicine pouches are worn around the neck, Charles explained that some people carry them in their cars for protection, tying them around the mirror and letting them dangle. I wanted to make more medicine pouches for my friends, so I took the class again the next day.

Charles Little Old Man and Marcelline Shoulder Blade were back, but we had a new group of students. One of the students was Rosalia Bad Horse. She was also known as Miss Northern Cheyenne Princess, a title she competed for and won in the 4th of July Powwow, one of the biggest powwows in the area. Young women from all over compete by performing dances and giving speeches. Rosalia shared with me another title that she received, Junior Miss Cheyenne 2006-2007. With that title she was invited to perform at the biggest powwow of them all, Gathering of Nations Powwow in Albuquerque, New Mexico. She said it was one of the highlights of her life. She said that so many people wanted to take a picture of her that she felt like a celebrity. I didn't realize it then, but Rosalia would play a very big part in helping me understand why I was led to the reservation.

That night when the activities had died down, I was able to take a quiet walk around the campus. It was starting to get a bit nippy, so I wore my new Eddie Bauer jacket that Eufemia gave me before I left. The chill in the air was only a small foreshadowing of the most brutal winter that lay ahead.

Friday was the last day of celebration for Native American Week at the school. The festivities began in the school's auditorium when one of the elders told the audience "A Crow Story" that illustrated the power of a child. It was called "A Crow Story" because it came from the Crow tribe. The elder spoke:

> "This is the story of a boy who saved his tribe. Every time he ate he would always take a little bit of the buffalo fat and feed it to the little turtle charm that hung from the chain that he wore around his neck. The little boy remembered that all creatures come from the Creator and he showed his respect to the Creator by giving the turtle a little bit of buffalo fat every time he ate. There came a time when the buffalo were nowhere to be found. No matter where the Indians hunted they could not find the buffalo. They called for the Medicine Man to pray for the return of the buffalo, but no one had the buffalo fat that the Medicine Man needed to perform the ceremony. Thereupon the little boy spoke up and said that he had always saved a little buffalo fat every time he ate. He removed the buffalo fat from the pendant he wore around his neck and gave it to the Medicine Man. The Medicine Man used the buffalo fat for the ceremony to call forth the buffalo. After the ceremony, the little boy laid his ear to the ground and suddenly he could hear the hoofs of the buffalo. He got

up and told the tribe not to worry, that the buffalo would soon come back. Shortly after that, the buffalo returned and the Indian tribe was saved all because of one little boy."

Everyone applauded as the elder encouraged the little ones in the audience that they too could have a huge impact on their tribe.

One of the very first things I noticed about the school was the buffalo heads. Several of them hung in the hallways and in the dormitories. I wasn't sure if they were real or not, but one of the security guards told me, "Oh, yeah, they're real all right." I had never worked at a school where there were buffalo heads sticking out of the walls.

After "A Crow Story," everyone headed outside for the parade. The parade started at Highway 212 and arrived at the school by 9:30 a.m. Students lined the main sidewalk of the campus as they anxiously waited for the procession to begin. Finally, four men each carrying a flag — the U.S. flag and three tribal nation flags, entered the grounds. A truck hitched to a flatbed with a teepee on top came next with Native Americans dressed in full regalia. Next in line was the fire engine truck with students taking a prominent place on top. The fire engine was followed by parents pulling little red wagons with children waving to the crowd. Students from the Crow tribe walked in unison carrying their class poster illustrated with their flag and tribal designs. Next in line was the second group of wagons carrying the youngest of the reservation. Each wagon was decorated with brightly colored balloons, yellow and purple, the school colors.

Following behind them each high school grade featured a car or truck with representatives from Senior, Junior, Sophomore, and Freshman classes in that order. Each class decorated their vehicle; some with posters that the students had designed and some with Native American blankets.

We did have a celebrity in our midst — Smokey the Bear. The U.S. Forest Service sponsored a truck with a sign across the front that declared "Preventing Wildfire is Good Business." Standing on a platform that was hitched to the truck, Smokey waved to the crowd. Topping off the parade was a cavalcade of Native Americans beautifully dressed in their regalia mounted on horseback. The eight horses with shiny coats and a diverse array of markings and colors made the parade extra special.

Following the parade, everyone headed over to the groundbreaking ceremony for the new dormitory that was beginning construction. The school provided boarding facilities for the students since most of them lived quite a distance from the school. Students would get to school on Monday morning with enough clothes and personal essentials to last them for the week and then they would leave for the weekend on Friday afternoon. I always thought that was so brave of them. I knew I could never leave home at that age and live in a dorm. I never even lived in a college dorm, but the students seemed to adapt to dorm life pretty well. While the current dorms were adequate, the school's enrollment was growing, so a new one was necessary and they had the money to build it.

The groundbreaking ceremony for the new dormitory began when the elders smudged the area with sage. Following the smudging, several speeches were given by school administrators and Father Paschal gave the final blessing of the dorm site. The drummers ended the ceremony with the Honor Song.

After the groundbreaking ceremony, we headed back to the main campus for a tepee raising contest between the Northern Cheyenne and Crow tribes. There were many other activities including Northern Cheyenne and Crow hand games, an arrow-throwing contest, and a number of booth displays including "A Cheyenne Lady's Dance Outfit Show," "Cheyenne Rattles," "Native Herbal Medicine," and "Meat Cutting."

The activities were followed by a buffet feast in the school's dining hall, but it wasn't much of a feast for me. I passed on the meat stew, although I heard it was delicious. I had a piece of bread and a boiled potato. Living in Montana was a real test of my commitment to being a vegetarian. But what I lacked for in terms of food was made up for in terms of knowledge. After I passed through the buffet, I found a seat next to my teacher and colleague, Ken Kania. Earlier in the month I had signed up for a history class, The History of the Cheyenne People, at Chief Dull Knife Community College. Ken Kania was the instructor and he was truly a remarkable teacher. I was so impressed with his ability to rattle off historical facts and events as if he was an eyewitness. He never used slide presentations. He had it all in his head. He didn't just lecture, he would weave fascinating stories, both historical and current throughout his talk. He was a bit folksy, which made him even more endearing.

Ken was also a history teacher at the school. He came shortly after college and with the exception of a one-year stint in Mexico, he spent his entire teaching career, which spanned forty years, on the reservation. He used to tell his students "You can't fool me. I know all your tricks and your fathers' tricks and in some cases your grandfathers' tricks." His classroom was right next to mine. During lunch I would go into his room to use his microwave. He always had a long list of comprehensive notes on the board that I sat and copied.

Ken possessed a vast extensive knowledge of the history of the Northern Cheyenne people. He also knew the background of many of the people living on the reservation. He told me that Charles Little Old Man, who had taught me how to make medicine pouches, at one time was the Sacred Hat Keeper for the Northern Cheyenne. That was a highly respected position responsible for care of the Sacred Hat, the buffalo cap and the horns used in healing ceremonies. There is even a designated Sacred Hat Tepee set aside for the keeping of the Sacred Hat.

The next day, Saturday, was our class field trip. Even though I had already gone to the Battle of Little Bighorn site, I was excited about going again. Ken was a wealth of information.

Ken told me:

> "Gold had been found in the Black Hills and the Indians weren't going to give it up. They didn't even feel like they owned it to sell, but since they were living there the U.S. had

offered them $60 million. They turned it down. After the Civil War, the U.S. government focused their attention on western expansion. Plans were underway to build a railroad. The government had given the railroad companies land to build and the railroad companies, in turn, were selling the land to Europeans. Twenty miles north and twenty miles south of the railroad tracks were up for sale. There were also people coming back from the California Gold Rush. Many hadn't found any gold, but on the way back they thought of settling on the Great Plains. The U.S. government also offered land to veterans of the Civil War. All of this was in the name of progress, but the Indian was in the way, literally. President Grant had given the Indians the ultimatum to report to the reservation by January 31, 1876. Sitting Bull, who was the leader of the Sioux, responded by saying it was impossible to do this. It was the dead of winter and it would be too difficult for women and children to pack up and move to the reservation. That response led to the government's policy of attack against the Indians. That attack would happen on June 25-26, 1876. It was a victory for the Sioux, led by Sitting Bull, but while the Indians won the battle they would eventually lose the war."

Ken continued:

"After the Battle of the Little Bighorn, U.S. policy changed drastically toward the Indian. Before the Civil War, the U.S. government had followed a policy of treaty-making and treaty-breaking; now the government took a hard line. Not that treaty-breaking wasn't a hard line, but now the U.S. policies were even more severe. The Indians would be rounded up, put on reservations and 'Christianized.' Christian missionaries were sent to the reservations, but they weren't very Christian. One of their worst practices was cutting the Indians' hair, which in Indian culture is sacred and a source of strength. It was traumatic. Missionaries often berated the Indians' religious practices, banned many of their ceremonies, and filled them with the fear of hell if they didn't convert to Christianity. Many of the Indians were not even given an education. They were simply given menial tasks to keep the reservations operating."

Following our conversation, we went outside for the last event of Native American Week, the powwow, the grand finale to an amazing three-day tribute. I looked out at the expansive campus filled with Natives wearing colorful clothes, feathers, ribbons, and headdresses. I took a bunch of pictures and then I saw Rosalia. She looked stunning dressed in her regalia and wearing her Northern Cheyenne Princess Sash. I asked her if I could get my picture taken with her and I was honored when she said yes.

The powwow lasted for hours. It was a spectacular sight, yet in the midst of it all I couldn't believe where my life had taken me. It was still hard for me to accept that I was living on an Indian reservation. I thought to myself, 'When this powwow is over, I'm not going home. This is my home.'

That night, I came home and wrote down as much as I could remember from my conversation with Ken, and all that I had experienced that week. I had started keeping a journal since coming to the reservation. Writing gave me a sense of purpose. Plus, I didn't want to forget all that I was learning.

The next morning everyone from Ken's history class met in front of the school and piled into the van and then we were off to the Little Bighorn Battlefield. I thought back to when I came up for my interview and made a quick stop thinking it would be the only chance I would have to visit it. I guess there was more for me to learn about Native American history and tradition than I could learn in one afternoon. Strange how life happens.

Once we arrived, we followed Ken to the site of Custer's Last Stand. As Ken began describing the bloody battle, my mind immediately began to wander. I looked out on the endless horizon. It was miles and miles and miles of Montana's wide open green lush landscape set against its big blue sky. I thought back to when I was leaving Los Angeles. My balcony was filled with a variety of succulents I had collected over the years that I didn't want to part with. My beautiful garden, that had taken so long to cultivate, had to go. I gave all my plants to Holy Spirit Retreat Center in Encino knowing that the Sisters would take care of them, but it was still hard for me to give them up. And now as I looked out at the immense panorama before me I realized I hadn't lost a thing. I gave up a little tiny balcony of potted plants for a breathtaking view of the Great Plains. It was a pretty good trade-off.

I stood in awe at the magnificent site before me as I listened to Ken's description of the Battle of Little Bighorn, what the Indians called Greasy Grass:

"Here was one of the last armed efforts of the Northern Plains Indians to try and hold on to their land. Custer, the hero of the Civil War and leader of the 7th Calvary fought against the Sioux, Cheyenne, and a band of other tribes. Led by Sitting Bull and Crazy Horse, the Indians were victorious while Custer met his end."

Ken explained that Custer's Last Stand was the battle that busted open hostilities between the U.S. government and the Indians. The year was 1876. Back East, they were celebrating the country's centennial when word reached them that Custer, the great Civil War hero, had been killed at the Battle of Little Bighorn. And so began the long years of war and hostilities with the Indians that finally came to an end at the Battle of Wounded Knee in 1890.

We left the battlefield and headed for Sheridan, Wyoming and had lunch at the Sheridan Inn, a National Historical Landmark. It was a great opportunity to connect with the other teachers who were on the trip and to get to know them a little bit better. Rarely do you get the opportunity to do that once the school year gets going, so I really appreciated the time and effort that Ken took to make it happen.

From 1894-1902 the inn was known as the W.F. Cody Hotel Company, named after one of its owners, William Frederick "Buffalo Bill" Cody, who sat on the porch of the hotel and auditioned acts for his Wild West Show. The show was about life in the West featuring Indian culture and the western way of life. Sitting Bull would eventually join the act and travel around the U.S., Canada, and Europe. The main attraction in the hotel is the saloon. The third barstool was used by Buffalo Bill himself. The original front desk and the original key boxes are still a part of the hotel lobby. Some famous people who visited the inn were Will Rogers, Ernest Hemingway, Bob Hope, Calamity Jane, and Herbert Hoover. I got all that from the hotel's brochure.

After lunch we headed for more battlefields: the Wagon Box Fight Site, the Fetterman Battlefield, and Fort Phil Kearny State Historic site. The Wagon Box Fight was a type of Alamo. A few whites were having a woodcutting party when they were attacked by Indians. The accompanying soldiers were few in number, but they were able to keep the Indians away. The cavalry was not as lucky at the Fetterman site. That battle was the worst defeat experienced by the U.S. Army during the Indian wars up until the defeat of Custer.

While I was at the Fetterman Battlefield, I visited the bookstore. I had heard the name Black Elk in recent weeks and since I didn't know that much about him, I bought *Black Elk Speaks* and *The Sacred Pipe — Black Elk's Account of the Seven Rites of the Oglala Sioux*. *Black Elk Speaks* had gained wide attention in the 1930s when the book was first published and then again in the 1960s. The book was about Black Elk's vision and it was still relevant almost a hundred years later. Ken assigned a project for the end of the semester, so I did mine on Black Elk. I studied his vision and did a collage type poster that depicted his encounter with the Six Grandfathers. The grandfathers welcomed him and told him to have no fear and that he was being called to teach. One grandfather gave him a cup filled with water that granted life to all, while another grandfather gave him a bow and arrow that had the power to destroy. Another grandfather gave him a red stick that represented the tree of life. He instructed Black Elk to teach people to care for the tree of life. There is much more to Black Elk's vision, but the core of the lesson was to respect life and to stay on the good path.

CHAPTER TEN

BATTLE OF LITTLE BIGHORN REVISITED

I had been on the reservation for a little more than a month. I had gone to powwows. I had celebrated Native American Week. I was taking a course in The History of the Cheyenne People at Chief Dull Knife Community College. I had an incredible time on Ken's field trip to the Battle of Little Bighorn and the Historic Sheridan Inn and the Fort Phil Kearny State Historic Site. While I was experiencing all these great things on the outside, on the inside I still carried around with me that feeling of discontent, lack of peace, an inner gnawing. I just couldn't shake it. No matter what I did, I still had this very disconcerting feeling inside of me.

Something else happened that made me feel uneasy. Late one night I noticed the security truck driving by my window. I peered out from behind the blinds. Even though it was dark, I noticed someone running around the back of my neighbor's house. The security guard never caught up with him. It scared me to think that somebody could be lurking around my house while I was sleeping. For that reason I always kept the doors locked and the DVD player on. And I never wore pajamas. I always slept in my jeans. I felt safer sleeping in my jeans. They were comfortable jeans though, old and soft with holes in them. Isn't that weird that I always wore my jeans to bed?

There was one bright spot. Andrew, my student from Santa Maria de las Rosas High School, had given me his email address before I left. I emailed him when I got to Montana to try to explain to him what had happened. I began to look forward to his emails. They were so kind and encouraging. It was so different from what I was experiencing on the reservation. My students here didn't seem to connect with me. One time I was walking up to the store and I passed by one of my students. I looked at her, smiled and said "Hi!" She walked right by me and didn't say a word. I thought, 'how strange.' I thought back to my old days at Santa Maria de las Rosas when I would walk across the campus and a student would yell out, "Ms. Wagner, I love you!" Now my students just walked right by. Another time I ran into one of my students at the Trading Post. Right away I acknowledged her and said, "Hi!" She looked at me almost like she didn't even know me and said a faint "Hi" back. It was like that in the classroom too.

Even though I incorporated a lot of different activities into my classroom and I encouraged my students to be as creative as possible, here on the reservation my "style" wasn't working. Whenever I tried something new or creative, students would say, "This is dumb. This is stupid." I would think, 'NYU is stupid?' I had learned all my strategies at NYU, but they weren't resonating with my students.

But no matter what they said, I never lost it. My 5th period class was the most difficult. One particular day will always stand out for me. The lesson could have been called "The Battle of Little Bighorn Revisited." Like I had done in so many other classes, I asked my students to clear their desks so we could have a quiet meditation time without any distractions. One girl refused. I asked her again very politely to please move her books off her desk. Her desk was her own little battlefield and she wasn't going to budge. It was almost as if it were a hundred years ago and I was telling her to move on to the reservation.

One student blew up at me, telling me that I didn't know how to talk to students. "You think you're going to come up here to our reservation and tell us how to act? You don't come here and tell us what to do."

I responded calmly, "All I said, was clear your desks. I didn't raise my voice or yell. I very respectfully asked her to clear her desk. The other students cleared their desks."

Another student chimed in, "She's having a bad day. Haven't you ever had a bad day?"

"I've had a couple," I replied.

And then another student, "You think you can come up here from Los Angeles and tell us what to do. This isn't LA."

The other students just watched, waiting to see how I would I respond. They wanted a fight, but they weren't going to get one.

It had been this way for weeks, never letting up. They would argue with me every opportunity. It was a battle every day and it culminated that day with this outburst.

Then I did something that I had never done in my entire career. I walked out of the classroom. There was a small hall adjacent to my classroom with a small bathroom off to the side. I went in there and just broke down and cried. I looked at myself in the mirror and I didn't even recognize myself anymore. I looked so sad and hopeless. I slapped cold water on my face, wiped my eyes and walked back into the classroom. It was as though I had never even left. No one cared.

You, the reader probably think I was being overly sensitive, but I had never had this problem before with kids. At Santa Maria de las Rosas, students would have asked, "Ms. Wagner, are you okay? You look like you have been crying? Is everything okay?" But here, it didn't matter. I don't even remember what I taught that day, except never to respond with anger. There were times of self-doubt and despair that I felt in the classroom, but one thing I made certain of, I never showed any anger. It was a lesson they would never forget and neither would I.

It was unusual for me to go to the dining hall for lunch. I liked to hunker down in my classroom and watch something on the internet, but when I heard grilled cheese sandwiches and tomato soup were on the menu I dashed over. I ran into Cameron, one of my students, and he asked me if I wanted to sit with him at lunch. This was the day after my "Battle of Little Bighorn Revisited."

"Well, this is unusual. Most students want to argue with me. You really want to sit down and have lunch with me?"

Cameron laughed, "Don't let a bunch of little savages get to you, Ms. Wagner."

So once I got my grilled cheese sandwich, I grabbed a seat next to Cameron. He was in the tenth grade, very knowledgeable and very serious about his spirituality and he was willing to answer all the questions I had. I was very interested in hearing his version of the Sundance. I had seen *A Man Called Horse* with Richard Harris, decades ago and I never forgot that last scene, but I wondered why anyone would do that. Cameron was eager to explain why.

"First, one has to prepare for a Sundance a year in advance."

"How do you do that?" I asked.

"Fasting, prayer, no alcohol for an entire year. It's a commitment."

"Then what happens?"

"The Sundance usually takes place in August, the hottest month of the year and lasts for about three or four days. The sun dancers stay out in nature all night long, fasting and praying for a vision. The last day of the Sundance they pierce themselves."

"Pierce themselves? How?"

"They use an awl. It's a pointed instrument that they use to pierce the skin above the nipple and then a skewer of bone is inserted through the piercing. Long rawhide strips are tied to both ends of the bone and then the strips are tied to the cottonwood tree. Then the dancer prays and dances around the tree until the rawhide rips the flesh."

"It sounds so brutal. Why do people do it?"

"Because it's powerful. It gives strength. Sitting Bull went into a Sundance right before the Battle of Little Bighorn. He was pierced one hundred times and we won that battle. That's something that the white man doesn't understand. Our warfare is connected to our spirituality."

The bell rang and it was time to go back to class. I told Cameron that I was going to go to the sweat lodge ceremony that night. As he got up to leave, he said, "Ms. Wagner, you can't go if you are on your moon."

"What?"

"I'm serious Ms. Wagner, you can't be on your moon," he said with authority.

I hadn't a clue what he was talking about and then it dawned on me. I cracked up laughing. I hadn't had a moon in years.

We had parent conferences that afternoon and you never know what to expect with a parent conference. This time I was in for a pleasant surprise. One of the parents was a doctor from Lame Deer. We chatted a lot about where we were from and how we ended up on the reservation. His words were very comforting and supportive. His wife came in shortly after and joined the conversation. While her husband worked at the clinic in Lame Deer, she worked at the school in the dormitory. She told me that the kids really liked me.

"What?" I replied. I couldn't believe it!

I thought she was saying that just to make conversation, but she insisted, "Yes, the kids really do like you."

"You've got to be kidding me. I thought they hated me."

She looked at me with reassurance, "Oh, no, they love you. They just don't say it to you, but I've heard them say it many times."

"They really do have a funny way of showing it," I said. I guess I was winning the battle after all.

CHAPTER ELEVEN

SWEAT LODGE

I was not on my moon, so I was able to go to the sweat lodge ceremony. I found out later the reason why a woman was not allowed in the sweat lodge during her monthly period. It had nothing to do with being unclean or impure. That time of month is considered a very powerful time in a woman's cycle, so powerful that it would upset the dynamic of the sweat lodge ceremony. I was glad I wasn't going to be upsetting the ceremony.

I had already gotten a preview of the sweat lodge. The previous Sunday right after mass, Faye, the one who kept sending me emails about coming up for an interview, was going to Heritage Living Center and asked if I wanted to go with her. I didn't have anything else to do, so I went along for the ride. The center was only a few miles from school. On the way up, Faye told me all about Father Emmett. He came to the reservation as a young priest in the 1950s with instructions to close the school down, but when he got here he was filled with compassion for the Northern Cheyenne people and saw the need to keep the school open. In addition to saying mass and hearing confessions, he was pretty savvy at raising money and he was able to turn the school around. I'm sure glad he did because God only knows where I would have ended up if I hadn't gotten hired. I'd probably still be working at Kiddie Kandids for eight bucks an hour.

Father Emmett retired from the school in 1994 after 40 years of service, but his work was not finished. In 1997 he founded Soaring Eagle, a Public Charity whose purpose was to build an assisted living center for tribal elders that would allow them to stay on the reservation and receive the care they needed. The Heritage Living Center, a state of the art facility, opened its doors in 2002 providing safe housing, nutritious meals and cultural activities for its residents. Among those activities was the sweat lodge ceremony that took place a short distance behind the center. As Faye and I made our way through the center and down the long hall we passed by a number of portraits of famous chiefs and sacred battle grounds.

Once outside, I spotted the sweat lodge a few yards in the distance. I had read about the sweat lodge and I had seen pictures, but I still didn't have a clear understanding of what it was or how it worked. The lodge itself was circular and only about four feet high. The frame was made of sturdy, yet flexible tree branches bent to create a dome-like structure and then covered with layers of blankets to keep the steam in and the light out. It could hold about twelve to fourteen people sitting comfortably on the ground. In the center of the lodge was a pit for heated rocks. Faye explained that rocks, both big and small, are collected earlier in the day and heated in another fire pit located just a few feet away from the lodge.

After the rocks are heated, and it takes hours, they are placed in the pit inside the sweat lodge. Everyone crawls in the sweat lodge, sits in a circle around the pit, and then the flap is closed. The leader pours water on the heated rocks which causes the steam. Typically, everyone stays in the sweat lodge for about fifteen to twenty minutes and then the leader opens the flap of the lodge and lets the cool air in and the hot air out. This is repeated four times. Each time the session gets a little bit hotter and lasts a little bit longer, with the last session being the most intense. Faye explained that some sweat lodge ceremonies can go on for hours depending on who is leading them. She told me the center conducted sweat lodge ceremonies every Wednesday.

That Wednesday, I got a ride up to the lodge with the JVCs. The JVCs, also known as the Jesuit Volunteer Corps, is an organization of young Catholics who have committed a year of their life to serving in communities of need throughout the United States and abroad. This group of volunteers chose to work on an Indian reservation in Montana. Their living arrangements were different than mine. They shared their living quarters, ate together, prayed together, and they had a van for transportation. Being good Catholics, they gave me a ride to the sweat lodge.

When we got there one of the JVCs was placing the heated rocks from the outdoor fire pit into the sweat lodge. He did this using a pitchfork. He had done the hard work of collecting the rocks earlier in the day and then setting them in the fire pit to be heated.

I had to prepare for the sweat lodge too. A few days before, I had gone to the thrift shop near school and gotten a pair of yellow and white checkered shorts and a white cotton T-shirt. I wore them under my jeans and sweater. Once I got to the center, I stopped in the restroom, stripped down to my shorts and T-shirt, wrapped a towel around me and then headed to the sweat lodge.

Even though Faye had explained the sweat lodge to me a few days earlier, I was filled with "what ifs." What if I collapsed? What if all of a sudden I started getting heart palpitations? Or worst case scenario, what if I died? A couple of people had died the year before in a sweat lodge in Arizona, so it could happen. Even though all these fears ran through my mind, I still wanted to do it.

We all crawled into the lodge and sat in a circle huddling the fire pit. There were about ten of us. Once the chief closed the flap to the lodge it was pitch black. Whether my eyes were open or closed, it was still pitch black. I couldn't see a thing. Even if I placed my hand right in front of my eyes, I still couldn't see it. It was the darkest place I had ever been in. I started to think of the sweat lodge as symbolic for where I was in my life. I didn't understand why I was in Montana. What was I doing here? Why was I here? I couldn't "see" the reason for it.

The chief poured water on the rocks and steam filled the lodge. I began to sweat immediately. Then the men began praying and chanting. I tried chanting along with them as best I could, but the only words I could understand were Wakan-Tanka, which meant Creator. A few prayed for special intentions.

I didn't say it out loud, but my prayer was that I would make it through the first session without passing out. If I passed out I would have been so embarrassed. I just sat there cross-legged and prayed that I would make it through the first round and if it got too intense

I would sit out for the rest of the sessions and just tell everyone that once was enough. After about fifteen minutes, the flap was lifted and a cool breeze filled the lodge. I made it through the first round. I was confident that I could go another one. More heated rocks were placed in the fire pit and then the flap closed again.

Round two — more prayers. Since I made it through the first round, now I could pray for someone or something and not worry about passing out. I thought about Dolores. She had driven me and my three cats fifteen hundred miles in a U-Haul up to Montana. If I was going to pray for anyone it would be her. I began to pray for her in my heart. She is one of the most selfless persons to ever come into my life. Her life had not been easy. She was divorced with five kids; four had been diagnosed with autism. The twins, Nicky and Nolan, 25, and Valerie, 20, were living in group homes. Natalie, 23, who was very high-functioning, lived at home with Dylan, 18, the youngest of the five who was not autistic. Dolores worked at a senior center and coordinated the meal program for homebound seniors. It was in her nature to always take care of other people, so now in my small way I would pray that somehow, some day all her kind acts would come back to her.

The flap opened and light and air came into the lodge. This time we crawled out of the lodge. It felt good to be out in the cold. I had never experienced such extreme contrasts before, going from hot to cold, sounds to silence, confinement to a wide open space. I had just been encased in a sweltering pitch black environment filled with chanting and now in the coolness of the night, surrounded by silence, I was enraptured by the limitless sky filled with what seemed like a million twinkling stars. For a moment it was heaven on earth and then we all crawled back into the darkness for round three.

As I took my place around the fire pit, I remembered the year before teaching a chapter on the pro-choice/pro-life movements in my morality class. I didn't want to bang my students over the head with a bunch of gory pictures of abortions or make any critical judgements of women who find themselves in that position. Instead, I had them write an essay, "A Day in the Womb." They had to imagine what it was like when they were a fetus in the womb. They had to write about their experiences — their feelings, the sounds they heard, and the sensations they felt. It was one of my most original and creative assignments. I was amazed at the honesty and sincerity of what my students wrote about — hunger, fear, comfort, wonder. Each essay was personal, reflective, and honest. Some were even humorous.

As I sat in the sweat lodge, I thought this must be what it is like to be in the womb — dark, hot, noises all around. I started to think about my mother. I missed her. She had died twenty-five years ago… from cancer. And while her memory was always there, now in the sweat lodge, I felt very close to her. I wondered what she would think of me living on an Indian reservation.

Later the chief explained that in the Cheyenne tradition, the sweat lodge is a type of womb. It is very hot and dark, but once the flap opens, one emerges as a new being ready to greet the world in a new way and ready to embrace new experiences. It was just like on the poster I had of the Native American on horseback looking up to the horizon with the words, "Face the future with an open heart…. Seek new experiences with an open mind…. Embrace your destiny with open arms." I was beginning to embrace my destiny. The flap opened. Cool air came into the lodge. After ten minutes the flap would close again for the last time.

Round four — the last round would be the hottest. This time the women prayed out loud. Many of their prayers were for family members or for friends who were going through a difficult time. When it was my turn to pray out loud, I told them that I was thankful for the people there who had welcomed me into their tradition. I prayed for my students; the ones that I had now and the ones that I had left at my old school and I prayed for all of the other students I had taught throughout the years. Then it got really, really hot. My heart started palpitating. I thought I was going to die. I thought about all the times when I wanted to die, when things didn't go the way I wanted them to go and I just got sick of living. Now I was thinking 'No, not yet. I'm not ready yet. I still have so much more to do.' The heat got so intense, I couldn't even pray. I was almost in a trance. Every time the chanting died down, I thought 'Okay, it's over,' and then they would start chanting again.

Finally, the flap opened. I was so relieved that I had made it through the entire ceremony without passing out. I crawled out of the lodge and I looked up again at the starlit sky. It was even more beautiful than before. I was so thankful not just for the sweat lodge, but for everything, for life itself. I was even thankful for the priest who had me fired from Santa Maria de las Rosas. If it wasn't for him I never would have had this experience. Sometimes you just want to go back to all those people who screwed you over and say, "Thank you."

After the sweat lodge, I went back to the restroom, changed my clothes, and met the rest of the group in the dining hall. We had a potluck waiting for us. It was part of the sweat lodge tradition. That night I slept like a baby.

The next Sunday, I headed back to the Heritage Living Center. I wanted Father Emmett to bless the medicine pouches I had made during Native American Week before I sent them to my friends. It was an incredibly hot day for this time of year and I was wondering why I was even walking the distance just to have Father Emmett bless a couple of medicine pouches. I was hoping that someone would stop and give me a ride and finally someone did. A teacher from the elementary school picked me up and gave me a ride right to the door of the center.

I went straight to the reception area and I asked if Father Emmett was around and if he could bless my medicine pouches. The Indian at the desk told me that Lee Lone Bear was coming to see Father Emmett and that he could bless my medicine pouches too. I waited and waited and waited. I wondered if this was even worth it. Finally, Lee Lone Bear walked through the door. He was a tall man with a huge presence. Soon after, I was led back to the chapel where I met Father Emmett along with a few members of the staff. It seemed that I had stumbled into a Native American healing ceremony. We all sat in a circle as Lee Lone Bear began the sacred rite. After a few prayers, he took in his hands a small bowl of dirt and placed a pinch of dirt between his fingers and thumb. With this he told the group, "We came from dirt. We will return to dirt. By connecting with the dirt we are recharging our spirit."

He blessed Father Emmett first, then he blessed each one of us. There were eight of us and I was the last one to go up and get a blessing. Like all the others before me, I faced the East, as Lee Lone Bear took sweetgrass and blessed my right foot, right hand, left foot, left hand, body, and head. I was so grateful to have been included in the ceremony. Once the ceremony was over I introduced myself to Father Emmett and asked if he could bless my medicine pouches and he did. And so did Lee Lone Bear.

I went to school on Monday and I asked my student whose last name was Lone Bear, if he was related to Lee Lone Bear. He told me, "Yes, he is my grandfather and he is one of the holiest men on the reservation." He went on to tell me, "To have a holy man like that bless you is a real honor."

That afternoon I got a ride up to the post office and was able to get all of my medicine pouches in the mail. I sent one to Dolores, one to my cousin Jim in North Carolina, one to my friend Marian in California, and one to my friend Anne back in Massachusetts.

CHAPTER TWELVE

AMISH STORE

The sweat lodge wasn't the only cultural anomaly I took part in while I was on the reservation. A couple of days later, Carole came over to my classroom and asked me if I wanted to go with her to the Amish store. The store was like no other store I had ever been to. It was run by an Amish family and while they kept to themselves they stuck out like a sore thumb every time they went someplace. Their horse and buggy was a gentle reminder of an earlier time when speed wasn't the goal in life. Every time I saw them coming in my direction I always wanted them to pick me up and give me a ride, but they never did. Maybe it was against their religion.

As for their dress, the men were always dressed in black and white with a matching black rim hat while sporting long, well-groomed beards. The women were fully covered with plain dresses and white aprons with bonnets on their heads. They came all the way from Minnesota by horse and buggy. I don't know what route they took, but it had to have been scenic.

We had gone up to the Amish store several times already, but this time the kids were in the yard. They must have been playing in the dirt all day. It was all over their faces and their clothes, yet they were the happiest group of kids I had ever seen in my life. No television, no video games, no internet, no cell phones, no social media, just playing outdoors. It reminded me of the healing ceremony I went to with Lee Lone Bear a few days earlier and his comment that dirt was sacred in the Native American tradition. And now here I was looking at these little kids with dirt all over them. They seemed to have found the key to happiness, playing in the dirt. I was reminded of that scripture verse when Jesus called a little child to him and then told the crowd that they wouldn't stand a chance of getting to heaven unless they became like children. I guess I should roll around in the dirt every once in a while if I want to get into heaven.

I asked the oldest, "What is your name?"

"I'm Mary." She pointed to her siblings, "And this is Anna, Barbara, and Adam."

"What did you do today?" I asked.

Mary was the spokesperson for the group. "We had school."

"Where is your school?"

"It's in the back of the store."

"What did you study today?"

"We studied English and German. And then we took care of the animals."

"What animals do you take care of?"

"We have goats, cows, hens, roosters, dogs, cats, ponies, and horses."

I looked around the area. The animals were grazing not too far from where we were. I told Mary I wanted to come back and take some pictures to which she replied, "You can come back and take pictures of the animals, but not us."

After our conversation, Carole and I went inside. Rebecca, the storekeeper, was always pleasant and friendly, but what I loved about her most was her down to earth spirit. Her pioneer dress and make-up free style was a refreshing change from the plastic surgery, Botox, and lipo that I was used to seeing in Los Angeles. It was late in the day and the sun was about to go down. Knowing that the Amish didn't use electricity I thought the store would be closing before we finished shopping, but Rebecca brought out a couple of kerosene lamps and we waved them up and down the aisles as we walked through the store scanning the shelves for deals. The store had everything from canned goods to household supplies, pet food, and a couple of hand-carved rocking chairs. Most of the canned goods had fallen off food trucks and had dents in them or they were a few days past the expiration date, so everything was discounted. With prices like .50 for a can of soup or .25 for a bottle of salad dressing, $20 could buy a week's supply of groceries. Once we finished our shopping, Rebecca totaled our goods. Another advantage, there was never a long line at the register. After we paid her, Carole and I headed back to the rez.

CHAPTER THIRTEEN

LEARNING TO LIVE WITHOUT

The Amish weren't the only ones without a car or television. Not having a car was my biggest adjustment, but it did have its advantages. I didn't have to pay for gas or car insurance or repairs. And there were the health benefits too. One day when I was taking a shower I felt a muscle in the back of my leg. When I looked at the back of my legs in the mirror — I couldn't believe what I saw, or I should say what I didn't see. No cellulite! Now that was something to celebrate! Fifty-two years old and no sign of cellulite on the back of my legs!

While I didn't think I was having much success in the classroom, there was at least one student I made an impression on. At one of the sports rallies, a senior standing next to me asked if I liked teaching at the school. She caught me a bit off guard, but I responded with a quick "Yes, I do." And then I asked, "Do you like it here?" She told me she was happy to be graduating. And then she said, "You inspire me!"

I was so surprised. I wasn't even her teacher and I didn't know how I could have inspired her. So I had to ask why.

"Because you walk to school," she said. "All the other teachers who live in the village drive their cars, but you walk and that inspires me."

At least I inspired one student at the school! And it had nothing to do with my teaching. Well, I guess I was teaching — by example.

It's amazing how you can eliminate one thing from your life; something that you think you can't live without and then something else comes into your life, something that you never saw coming and it makes your life a lot more rewarding and satisfying. Not having a car was good for my health and it truly brought friendship into my life. Whenever someone was making the two-hour trip to Billings or the hour or so haul to Sheridan, I tagged along. It was the perfect opportunity to share thoughts, problems, dreams of the future, or even to decide where to go to get something to eat. No matter who I caught a ride with, I always enjoyed their company.

And who needs Starbucks? While I enjoyed stopping at Starbucks whenever I was in Billings or Sheridan, and it did remind me of home, I had only indulged myself a couple of times since I had moved to Montana. So I was saving a few extra dollars to say the least.

Television, I can live without it! The deal for DISH TV was for a two-year contract and I didn't want to commit to two years. But I did have a DVD player and I watched the same videos over and over again. My video library consisted of *Apollo 13*, *Sea Change*, *Shawshank Redemption*, *The English Patient*, and Joseph Campbell's *Mythos*.

I didn't have the internet either. I did have access to the internet at school, so I wasn't totally removed from civilization. I always caught up on the news when I got to school in the morning and before I left at the end of the day.

Gelson's salad bar in Calabasas — now that was a tough one to give up, especially being a vegetarian. The Trading Post in town did have a produce section, but it was nothing like what I was used to. There were times when I would just stand there trying to decide which tomato I was going to buy, when there were a half a dozen to choose from. One day while I was standing in front of the produce section, the guy who worked there asked me, "Are you a vegetarian?"

"Yes, I am. How did you know?"

"I've seen you here before and I noticed that you always buy fruit and vegetables, never any meat. It must be really hard being a vegetarian in these parts."

"It's been a test, for sure."

"I'm in charge of the produce and since I know you're a vegetarian, I'll try to get as much in as I can." He said, "Wait, here."

A few minutes later, he came back with a small fruit and cheese plate for me. "Here, I just made this up for you, so you know it's fresh."

"Thank you so much. I really appreciate it." Now that's Montana hospitality. One of the things I loved about Montana was … everyone was your neighbor. There were no strangers, everyone helped one another out.

I hadn't done any shopping for clothes in months, except for the yellow and white checkered shorts and white T-shirt I bought at the thrift store to wear for the sweat lodge. I didn't really dress for looks in Montana. I dressed for warmth. Winter was setting in and I got into the practice of wearing two pairs of pants to school every day, just to keep warm.

I hadn't had my hair colored in months either. That was a first. I had been coloring my hair for so long I had forgotten what my natural hair color was. I think I missed my hair stylist Gail, more than anyone else. Not for sentimental reasons, but pure vanity. I went from being a Southern California bouncy blonde to a slicked back Montana brunette with a couple of grey strands in a few short months. To add to my misery, my hair extensions started falling out six weeks after I arrived. I ended up tying all of them together making a ponytail and wearing it to school every day. I let go of a lot of things when I came to the reservation, but I couldn't let go of my hair extensions.

I hadn't been to a nail salon in three months either. I really didn't need a pedicure, since I was wearing boots every day and I always wore socks to bed to keep my feet warm, so no one even saw my feet.

While I hadn't been going to the nail salon, I was going to weekly sweat lodge ceremonies and my skin was clear and glowing. My roots were black, my hair extensions had fallen out, my nails were a mess, but my skin was glowing and I didn't have any cellulite. I guess it was an even exchange.

CHAPTER FOURTEEN

VERIZON ON THE HORIZON

While I learned to live without a lot of my everyday conveniences, there was one other thing besides my hair extensions that I couldn't live without — a phone. I hadn't talked with anyone from home since I had gotten to the reservation. I had a cell phone when I came to Montana, but the carrier I was using didn't provide service on the reservation, only Verizon did that. I had put off making the change, but now it was inevitable. I called Verizon from the phone in my classroom and ordered a cell phone.

The next morning I got an email from Verizon informing me that my phone would arrive at 7:00 p.m. the next day at the school's address. Oh! No! That wasn't going to work. No one would be there at the school to sign for it. I had to call FedEx and see if they could change the delivery time. I spoke with Ted. When I gave him my tracking number and he pulled up my information, he recognized right away that I was on an Indian reservation.

"You're living on an Indian reservation?"

"Yes," I said.

"What do you do?"

"I'm a teacher."

"You're doing a really great thing. I hope you know that."

"What?"

"You're doing a really great thing."

"What do you mean?"

"Teaching those kids. That's awesome what you are doing. I live in Arizona and I know what the Indians have gone through. And I think you're doing a really great thing."

I wasn't expecting that. "Thank you so much for saying that. You made my day. You really did."

"Glad I could do that for you. I'm going to put a rush on this and make sure that you get your phone as soon as possible."

That night, my soul filled with new energy and enthusiasm, thanks to Ted. I was doing a really great thing here on the reservation. I was teaching. I kept going over what Ted had told me, that I was doing a really great thing. It's truly amazing the people who come into your life at just the right moment and suddenly your whole perspective changes.

The next day, I was waiting at home for my phone to arrive when I saw Faye pull into my driveway. When I opened my door, she called out to me, "Luella, did you get your package?"

"No," I told her.

"Get in the car, quick. I just saw the FedEx guy leaving the village."

"Oh! No!" Panic filled me. For the past few days, I had been so excited about getting my new phone, I didn't think I could go another day without one.

As soon as we got to school, I saw the FedEx truck. Faye stopped the car and just as I jumped out, the truck started to pull away. I ran down the street waving my hands yelling, "Stop! Stop!" I could see the driver looking in the rearview mirror. The truck came to a stop and I ran towards it. I finally caught up with him. "Do you have my phone?"

"Yes, I do."

"I was worried that you were going to leave without delivering my phone."

"I wasn't going to leave until I found you!" And then he handed me my phone.

I thanked him profusely for coming all the way out to the reservation. I was so happy I wanted to kiss him!

Verizon was more than just a phone, it was my lifeline. One of the first persons I called was my friend Jerry. It was good to hear his voice. We talked for hours. He was really surprised when I told him that I was living on an Indian reservation, but he wanted to hear all about it.

"Sorry I didn't get a chance to talk to you before I left."

"Left?"

"Yes, I left California."

"Why?"

"I got fired and the only job I could find in the entire country was working on an Indian reservation in Montana."

"Tell me all about it."

"My department chair screwed me over. It was so wrong. It was so unjust. I did everything they told me to do and the kids loved me. When I think back to all I did …"

"No, no, not that, tell me about the reservation."

"Oh, that, yes, yes, the reservation. Oh, Jerry! You wouldn't believe it! I live in a real tiny village. The population here is four hundred. I walk to school every day."

"What are the kids like?"

"They're all Indian; mostly Northern Cheyenne and Crow, but I have Lakota and Dakota Sioux, and a few Apache and Navajo."

"What reservation are you on?"

"The Northern Cheyenne on the Tongue River."

He started laughing. "That's hilarious."

"What's hilarious?"

He was still laughing.

"What's so funny, Jerry?"

"You. You — living next to the Tongue River. That's hilarious. You finally found your niche. You've traveled all over the world and you've finally found your place."

"What do you mean?"

"You're always talking. Ever since I have known you, you never shut up and now you're living next to the Tongue River. Are you going to be buried there? May your tongue rest in peace lying next to the Tongue River."

He was right. I love to talk and having a cell phone made all the difference in the world.

CHAPTER FIFTEEN

THE GRASSHOPPER, THE LABRADOR, AND JD

The weather was still nice and I loved the Montana colors. I hadn't seen leaves change color since I had left Massachusetts almost thirty years before, so it was a bit of a déjà vu experience for me. Each day as I passed the cottonwood tree that stood in front of my house I noticed the leaves change from green to golden yellow and then drop off until the entire tree stood bare. I somehow knew that the falling of the leaves and the approach of winter signaled the coming of one of the darkest periods in my life. Black Elk once said that the reason for the long cold winters is to help one forget about the past. I had a lot to forget about and even though I didn't want it, I knew that a long cold winter would probably be the best thing for me. Forgetting the past seems to be the best way of bringing in new opportunities and meaningful relationships, perhaps the only way.

As the days grew shorter and the nights grew colder, heat became an important part of my life on the reservation. Whether I was in the sweat lodge, my house, or in my classroom, I loved the heat. The first thing I did when I got to my classroom in the morning was to put the heat up. By the time 5th period came around, the kids would walk in and say, "Ms. Wagner, what are you running in here — a sweat lodge?"

One time when we were driving up to the sweat lodge, one of the Jesuit volunteers said, "We still haven't used our heat. We are trying to save money for the school." I was impressed with their willingness to sacrifice, but as long as they weren't using their heat I didn't feel guilty about using mine. The first thing I did as soon as I got home was turn the heaters up full blast. I didn't put the heat on in every room, just the living room where I spent most of my time. My cats loved it too. Juanita, my little tortoise shell, loved sitting by the heater. She was my littlest one. She weighed about seven pounds, but ate everything. And then there was my Tiger. He loved looking out the window, so I gave him a nickname — "He Who Looks Out Window." One time in the middle of the night, Tiger was peering out the window so intently I got scared. I thought someone might actually be out there. I got up real slowly and managed to get a peek at what he was staring at. And right outside my window was a lean long-legged deer staring right back at us. Being from Reseda, Tiger had never seen such a sight! That wasn't the only wildlife that crossed our path. We did see an occasional pheasant in the front yard every once in a while too.

And then there was my little Moo Moo, my stowaway. I used to put the heat up in her room too. A teacher told me that she had three dogs living with her in the village and they evicted her. That scared the shit out of me, so I had to be really vigilant about keeping Moo Moo hidden. I always kept the blinds closed in Moo Moo's master bedroom and I never had anyone over to the house, except for Carole. Every time she came over I was always afraid that Moo Moo would start meowing, but she never did. I worried about my cats the whole time I was there. The closest veterinarian was twenty miles away and I didn't have a car. I always worried that one of them would get sick and I wouldn't have any way to get them to the vet. Fortunately, they were healthy and happy the entire time we were in Montana.

Living on the reservation, away from all the traffic and noise, gave me the chance to connect with nature on a completely different level. In California, I always enjoyed going to the beach or taking an afternoon hike, but I always had to take the freeway to get there. Here on the reservation, my total existence was surrounded by nature — wide open space, the rolling hills, the big sky. I didn't have to seek it out.

I read a lot when I was on the reservation. One book I really came to love was *Mother Earth Spirituality* by Ed McGaa, also known as Eagle Man. He wrote about nature in spiritual terms, specifically the lessons that animals could teach us. I knew that when Indians went on a vision quest the appearance of an animal could have a special message meant just for them, but I never thought for a minute that an animal randomly crossing my path could add any significant meaning to my life. Eagle Man taught me that was not so. He wrote that even an insect could reveal something new to me. 'C'mon,' I thought, 'is that really possible?' I decided to try it out. I started to anticipate an animal, a bug, a bird coming into my life with a message that would somehow give me direction or at least give me a clue as to why I was on the reservation in the first place.

One day I was sitting outside on my backdoor steps waiting for Carole to pick me up. She was going to an animal shelter in Sheridan to adopt a Labrador Retriever and she asked me if I wanted to go with her. As I sat there waiting, I started to wonder if an animal was going to cross my path. It was the perfect opportunity. And then I thought, 'no animal is going to appear to me,' but all of a sudden I saw it! There it was! A little grasshopper right in front of me! I was so taken up with this little tiny creature. He jumped and hopped almost like he was showing off to me. I thought he was very brave, considering I could have ended it all with one swish. I watched how he continued to jump from one grass blade to another.

Okay, now what's the lesson? I sat there and thought about it. I started to think about all my years in education — this was my nineteenth. Even though I had achieved several remarkable years in teaching, the last few years had been dismal to say the least. It was depressing and it left me shattered. I was let go from one school because I didn't "fit in." Discouraged but not deterred, I bounced back and got another teaching job, but the school closed down after one year. Determined to teach, I found another teaching job, but after two years of my best teaching a priest had me fired because he didn't think I could teach.

Even though I had been rejected several times, I always found another school that wanted me. This time it was a mission school on an Indian reservation. I suddenly had the thought that I was a "grasshopper" teacher. I could jump from one school to another, one grade to another, even if it meant packing up a U-Haul and driving fifteen hundred miles, I could do it. It was in my nature to jump around. That was the lesson of the grasshopper! I didn't have anything to be ashamed of. I was as brave and agile as that little grasshopper and that was a good thing! Eagle Man was right. Even the smallest of creatures has infinite wisdom to pass along to us.

A few minutes later Carole drove up and we headed to Sheridan. We got to the shelter and I waited in the car while Carole went through the process of adoption for her new family member. After about an hour of waiting in the parking lot, Carole came walking out like a proud parent with a big black Labrador Retriever by her side. She opened the car door and he jumped in and greeted me with a warm, wet, slobbering tongue all over my face before he made his way to the back seat. He was excited about his new owner and a new home.

Before we headed back to the reservation, I asked Carole if we could stop at a liquor store. We were not allowed to buy alcohol in the village. It was written in the employee handbook. Some of the students worked at the Trading Post and if they saw a teacher buying alcohol it would set a really bad example. It just wouldn't look good. Now in Sheridan, this was my chance to pick up a bottle of liquor that would keep me company for a long winter's night.

We found a small liquor store on the outskirts of town and Carole waited in the car as I went in and browsed the aisles of the neatly displayed Merlots, Chablis, Cabernets, and Zinfandels. Wine was fine for sitting at a California bistro nibbling on a Caesar salad, but this was Montana. I needed something hard core, something intense to get me through the grueling cold that was ahead of me. I turned down another aisle and eyed the shelves of orderly arranged bottles of gin, vodka, tequila, brandy, and rum and then I found it — Jack Daniel's Old No. 7 Tennessee Sour Mash Whiskey. That was it! That was what I came in for! It went with the rugged Montana lifestyle.

I picked up a six-pack of Coke and headed for the cashier. As he rang up my order, he looked at me and with a quick wink asked, "A little JD to keep you warm, huh?" I chuckled, "Yeah, to keep me warm and to keep me company." I headed out to the car happy. Carole got a dog and I got my Jack Daniel's — that was the man that Edie predicted I would meet in Montana. Now I could settle in for a long cold winter.

Naturally, the following week would be Red Ribbon Week at school. I was familiar with Red Ribbon Week since most schools in California sponsor the event once a year.[1]

For the whole week students could choose from a series of workshops with topics ranging from Alcoholism, Domestic Violence, Suicide, Drug Abuse, and Cancer. The workshops were intense, honest, and heart-wrenching. The suicide rate in Montana was the second highest in the country, second to Alaska. I had already heard of a student suicide at a nearby school.

One of the workshops I attended was Heroin Addiction. The presenter was a recovering addict. Going over the effects that heroin had had on his life, at one point he said, "I could never hold down a job. The longest I have ever had a job has been four years."

I thought, 'That's longer than I've ever held down a job. I must look like I'm a drug addict on my resume.' Thank God I saw that grasshopper the other day or else I would have thought I was a total loser. I continued going to the workshops and learning all that I could about the struggles living on the reservation. By the end of the week, I needed a drink.

There was another reason for me to have a drink. It was a time of celebration for me. That week I got the letter from Sallie Mae:

Dear LUELLA WAGNER:

Congratulations! You've completely paid off the student loans starred below. We've enjoyed having you as a customer and wish you the best in the future.

You're welcome to visit us online at SallieMae.com or call us toll free at 888-2-SALLIE (888-272-5543) with any questions you may have. We are available Monday – Thursdays 8 a.m. – 8 p.m. Eastern Time.

We hope you'll keep us in mind for any future education financing needs and we appreciate the opportunity to serve you.

Sincerely,
Sallie Mae Customer Service

My mother would have been so proud. I did it. I paid off all my student loans. This was the last one. This was a big achievement for me. After I graduated from Boston University and moved out to California, my mother made it a point that she and my father were not going to pay off my student loans. "Your father and I don't have any money! We are on Social Security. We don't have any money to give you, so don't call us. You've graduated from college, so you can get a job and pay it off yourself. And when they call about your student loan, I am giving them your phone number, I'm telling them where you work, and where you live. Don't think for one minute that your father and I are going to pay off your student loans. You're paying them off yourself." She went over and over it until finally she calmed down. I didn't say a word. After she was done, my Dad called me into his room. He was sitting in his wheelchair and he motioned for me to come close and then he whispered, "Don't listen to your mother. If you need money, just call me and I will get it to you somehow. I'll figure something out. You can call me anytime, but just don't tell your mother. She doesn't have to know." That's what dads are for.

I went back to California and a year later I enrolled at UCLA and got my teaching credential, but I had to take out another loan. Once I had paid off that loan and my loan for Boston University, I took out another loan for my Master's Degree at New York University. This was the loan that I had finally paid off. I did it Mom, I paid off all my student loans, all by myself. Actually, it was a pretty good lesson for me. It taught me the value of an education and responsibility for paying off my debts. I celebrated with a little Jack Daniel's!

CHAPTER SIXTEEN

MY PHILOSOPHY OF EDUCATION

One of my friends always says, "You create your own reality." It was hard for me to accept that I had created the scenario of being fired, but after a lot of reflection and introspection, I finally came to the realization that I wanted to get fired. Well, I didn't really want to get fired, but I didn't want to stay at Santa Maria de las Rosas High School either. I was proud of the work that I had done and I loved my students, but I wasn't given any opportunities to grow, and my teaching stalled. Here on the reservation I was challenged in every way possible, but my anchor was my philosophy of education.

I have always remembered what a Buddhist nun told me years ago about teaching. I remember the conversation exactly. I had gone on and on about the lack of support from administration and then she looked at me and said, "Stop! Stop! Just go into the classroom and love your kids." Just go into the classroom and love your kids? Easy for her to say, but I started to think about it. What did that mean to really "love my students?"

I did some research. I came across the writings of St. Augustine. He dealt with the same discipline problems that all teachers have to deal with, and his advice was to always respond positively. If the student interrupted, the teacher was not to get angry or upset. The student still had consequences for bad behavior, but the teacher always corrected the students in a way that was edifying, rather than humiliating.

I decided to apply that philosophy directly to my teaching. Whatever the student did, I would always respond with patience and kindness. That meant that if a student needed a Band-Aid, needed to go to the bathroom, needed a pen, needed help with a problem, needed a tissue, I would respond kindly. If they interrupted my lesson, talked during class, came in late, or made any kind of fuss, I always demonstrated patience and refused to let it get the best of me. I never wanted them to see me angry and I never raised my voice. It was a challenge to be sure. I envisioned myself as a role model for behavior for my students. I behaved how I wanted them to behave.

While it was trying at first, eventually I had the students in the palm of my hand. I remember the day at Santa Maria de las Rosas, when one of my students said, "Ms. Wagner, you never yell at us." It's not unusual for teachers to yell or scream and when I was younger, that was my approach. Now, older and wiser, I got more from my students with a quiet tone of voice than a loud one. Plus, it didn't take as much energy out of me as yelling did.

I had tapped into something that I had never learned at UCLA or NYU. While I had learned a multitude of methodologies and strategies, I had discovered that the most effective way of implementing those strategies was with steadfast patience. At Santa Maria de las Rosas patience was my guiding force. It was the key to gaining students' attention and respect and then I got fired. And it all led to the reservation where my patience was tested beyond anything I had ever experienced in education.

On one particular day the kids just wouldn't shut up. Every single class, they would not shut up. No one was listening to anything I said. By the time 7th period came around, I just couldn't take it anymore. While I never yelled or got angry with the kids, on the inside I was fuming. It was a tough day. When I got home, I poured myself a Jack Daniel's.

While they didn't always listen to me, I always listened to them and whenever they wanted to share their stories, I was all ears. One day they were talking about a relay from Nebraska to Busby, Montana to commemorate the Fort Robinson Breakout.

They were eager to explain the Fort Robinson Breakout:

> "The Cheyenne were barricaded at Fort Robinson with no food, firewood, or water. Chief Dull Knife led the breakout

and while most were captured and brought back to Fort Robinson, Chief Dull Knife and a few others escaped. And every year it is remembered in a relay from Nebraska to Busby, Montana." [2]

I had taught a lot of students over the years and the one thing I noticed about my students on the reservation was they had an emotional connection to their history. They lived it. It wasn't a textbook or a homework assignment, it was their heritage and it was a proud heritage. It was in their blood. They carried it with them. I could sense a little hostility towards me for what had happened over a hundred years ago. I found myself saying, "It was wrong, what the white man did, but don't blame me for something they did. I'm trying to be part of the healing. I'm trying in my small way to make it up to you." One student spoke up, "We love you, Ms. Wagner." Finally! I was starting to get through! Normally, I start the school year off with a couple of icebreakers, but here on the reservation I had to wait quite a while for the ice to melt.

CHAPTER SEVENTEEN

THE INDIAN WHO TAUGHT ME A LESSON

A couple of days later I woke up only to see Tiger sitting like a statue staring out the window. "Tiger, what are you looking at?" He continued staring out the window, so I said it again, "Tiger, what are you looking at?" He didn't budge, so I made my way over to the window and what a beautiful sight — just like a Christmas card! The entire village was blanketed in a light snow. No wonder Tiger was mesmerized. He never saw anything like that in Los Angeles. But looking at it was quite different than walking in it.

I had boots — Southern California boots, not Montana boots. They were stylish trendy black boots with a slight heel, but they didn't have any traction. The only other shoes I had were my Nikes and they weren't meant for snow. So I ventured out into the snow-covered streets wearing my Southern California boots. I had gotten all the way to my classroom when I lost my balance, slipped, and went flying. 'Oh, my God! I hope nobody saw me!' At first I couldn't believe that I had taken a fall like that. I picked myself up and looked in every direction to make sure no one saw me. Later that day, I had to walk over to the administration building and I did it again — fell flat on my butt. I couldn't believe it! I asked God, "Couldn't you have sent me some angels or done *something* to stop me from falling?" I looked around again to make sure no one saw me and then I picked myself up and brushed myself off.

I guess humiliation was my fate because later that day as I was walking home, it happened again — this time in front of everybody. I had just walked past the school bus, when I slipped again and took another hard fall on my butt and all the kids on the bus saw me go down. A car was coming towards me and there I was smack in the middle of the road. No matter how hard I tried to pick myself up, I kept slipping and sliding all over the place. It was utter humiliation. I saw one of my students walking away as if he didn't even know me, but I yelled out anyway, "Trevor! Help me! Help me!" He turned around and I guess he felt sorry for me so he walked over and reached out his hand to help me up. I thanked him immensely, but he never said a word. That student never talked, even in my classroom. The funny thing is, I had his sister in class and she never stopped talking.

I crossed the street and made my way down the snow-covered hill to the village. I didn't know what hurt more — my wrists or my butt. Every time I had fallen down, I automatically used my wrists to break the fall and every time I hit the ground my butt fell on ice. I was in excruciating pain and it didn't help that I could hear my mother's voice calling down from the heavens, "Jesus fell three times, too."

"Oh! Shut up! I don't want to hear about Jesus!" And then I couldn't help it. Tears started streaming down my face uncontrollably. To make matters worse, it was so cold that my tears turned to little sheets of ice. "Why don't you make the priest who got me fired go through this? He's the one who should be punished, not me. You don't even know what you're doing, you stupid idiot."

Yep, that's what I said to God.

I spent the rest of the night in intense pain and agony. My wrists were swollen, my butt was sore and every muscle in my body ached. I was convinced that my wrists were broken and I was going to need to go to the hospital in the morning. The hospital was in Billings, a two-hour drive. I didn't have a car. Even if I did have a car, I couldn't drive myself because my wrists were so banged up. Another teacher would have to give me a ride and the principal would have to get a sub for two people. I lay on the couch, beaten and defeated. Everybody was right. It was too damn cold up here. I couldn't imagine myself staying for another seven months. I didn't have the strength, or the stamina, or the will to stick it out. And to think, I didn't even make it past the first snowfall.

That night I said a little prayer and it went like this: "Why don't you just kill me now? Go ahead, you can do it, just take my breath away. That's what you want, right? Go ahead, do it. Get it over with. Take my breath away."

I finally escaped my pain and misery and dozed off to sleep. When I woke up the next morning, I couldn't believe it! My wrists weren't broken. I moved them in all different directions and twisted them every which way and there was no pain. I didn't have to call in sick after all. I could go to school, pass out papers, type on the computer, and write on the board. I call it "the miracle in Montana."

Carole stopped by my classroom at lunch and asked me if I wanted to ride up to the post office with her. I jumped at the chance. A few days earlier I had ordered a pair of real Montana snow boots from the Sierra Trading Post and I was hoping that they had arrived. When we got to the post office, the counter inside was closed because the postal workers were having their lunch too. I checked my post office box and I had a notice that there was a package for me. I had to yell through the tiny opening of my post office box to the workers who were having their lunch to ask if I could possibly have the key to the larger post office box so I could get my package. Once I got the key, I unlocked the larger box and got my package. I opened it up like a little kid on Christmas morning, tearing through the tissue and reaching in for my new boots. I put them on right away. They fit like a glove. They matched perfectly with my Eddie Bauer winter jacket that Eufemia had given me. I walked out of the post office feeling like the time in second grade when my mother bought me my first pair of white go-go boots.

Later that day as I was walking home from school I heard someone yell, "Hey, hey…" Now picture this. I'm dressed in my Eddie Bauer jacket, my sweater, my scarf, my gloves, my two pairs of pants, and my newly acquired Montana boots, and across the street was a man standing on his porch wearing nothing but a T-shirt and a pair of shorts. I couldn't help but notice that one of his legs was a prosthetic.

"Hey, I see you walk by here all the time. What's your name?"

I looked at him and I said, "Well, before I came to the reservation it was Luella Wagner, now it's Luella Falls Down."

He started laughing, "Hey, that's a real Indian name. Did you know that?"

"Yeah, I know. That's why I took it. I kept on falling down, so I just thought it made sense to take that name."

"You always walk by here so fast, by the time I get to the door, you're already gone. I have always wanted to invite you in. Do you have time?"

'Do I have time?' I thought to myself. 'I've got seven months.'

"C'mon over." he said.

As I crossed the street, I thought 'Okay, I get it, last night I was ready to die because I thought my wrists were broken, and now I meet a man who has one leg and it doesn't even faze him.'

As I entered his home, he introduced me to his wife and his kids. He invited me to his art studio where he showed me his collection of beaded keychains, medicine pouches, knife sheaths, and purses. His beadwork was beautiful. Beadwork is done so meticulously and it takes so much patience. I was very interested in learning the art and I planned on taking a beadwork class at the Beadwork Institute the next semester.

He also told me that he was in a drum group and he gave me a copy of his CD to listen to. We talked for a very long time.

I really wanted to ask him, "Hey, aren't you pissed off at somebody? I couldn't help but notice that you have only one leg. What was it? A war injury? Did a drunk driver hit you? C'mon, you can tell me. Don't you want to tell me your hard luck story? Don't you want to dwell on it?" But I couldn't do it. I didn't want to ruin his joy. I wanted his joy.

So I asked him, "Hey, what makes you so happy?"

He told me that every morning when he woke up the first thing he did was to greet the sun and then offer the day up to the Creator. He talked of the Tongue River Valley and how the chiefs would go to the highest point and greet the morning light and ask the Creator for guidance and direction. He told me how he connected with nature through prayer and meditation. He was so happy talking about the Creator, meditation, his beadwork, and his music. Even though he had only one leg, it didn't stop him from doing what he was meant to do. I left a few hours later, a little wiser and a little more humble. I had a lot to learn on the reservation.

CHAPTER EIGHTEEN

STAGE THREE

It wasn't just in the classroom that I experienced hostility; it was also coming at me from the principal's office. I had gotten into the habit of staying at school late correcting and grading papers so I didn't have to bring them home with me. It was around 6:00 p.m. when I started walking home. It was dark, no one else was around. I thought I was the only one at school, until I saw the light on in the principal's office. He saw me walking by and he motioned for me to come in. I thought it was for a friendly "how are things going?" chat. I don't know what I was thinking because remember it's never good when you get called to the principal's office. I stood outside his office till he motioned for me to come in and take a seat.

"Where were you?"

"What do you mean, where was I? I was in my classroom correcting papers."

"Why weren't you at the meeting?"

"We had a meeting?"

"We had a stage three meeting after school today and you weren't there."

"Oh! I am so sorry. I never miss meetings. I guess it just slipped my mind or something. It isn't like me to miss meetings. I am really sorry. I assure you it won't happen again."

"Make sure it doesn't."

I left his office with a very sick feeling in my stomach. I couldn't believe I missed a meeting. I never miss meetings. I didn't remember getting an email about a meeting or even hearing another teacher talk about it. What on earth was a stage three meeting anyway? I had been in education for nearly twenty years and I had never heard of such a thing. I found out later that it was a parent conference and I wasn't the only teacher who missed the meeting, but I wasn't going to let it happen again. The next time I got an email for a stage three meeting, I printed it off and taped it right next to the wall by my desk so I wouldn't forget.

The day of the meeting the principal stormed into my classroom during my prep period, "Where were you?"

"What do you mean, where was I? I've been sitting here in my classroom correcting papers."

"You missed another meeting."

"What are you talking about? That's impossible. I have it right here." I grabbed the copy of the email that I had posted to the wall. "Look, I have it right here taped to the wall so I wouldn't forget it. It's after school, right?"

He looked at me and said, "Read the email again. It was this morning, before school." I looked at the email again and he was right. The meeting was before school. I had done it again. I missed another stage three meeting. What could I say?

"I am really sorry. When I got the stage three email I just assumed it was after school, like the last one. I am so sorry."

"Don't let it happen again," and then he stormed out.

You're not going to believe this, but … I missed another meeting. It was a few weeks later. I was walking home from school past the administration building when the principal called me over. He met me at the door.

"Where were you?"

"I was in my classroom correcting papers."

"Why did you miss another stage three meeting?"

I didn't even know there was one. He called me into his office, sat down at his desk, and methodically went through his emails. I felt like I was a prisoner at a parole hearing and it wasn't looking good. He showed me the email that went out the week before.

'Well a lot happens in a week,' I thought. I sat there in a daze. I didn't know what to say. Other than, "I'm really sorry."

And then he said something that I will never forget, "I just shake my head at you!"

He actually shook his head at me too. I went home and just wanted to crawl under a rock for the rest of the year.

I thought I was losing my mind. I felt like Jessica Tandy's character in *Driving Miss Daisy*. She was an eighty-year-old retired schoolteacher and she literally went nuts. There was one scene where she went through the house screaming "Where's my papers? Where's my papers?" Yeah, she really lost it and I was feeling somewhat the same. I must be losing my mind, but I was only fifty-two, not eighty-two!

You might think I was making a big deal out of nothing. I mean after all, every teacher has a couple of run-ins with the principal at some point in their career. But no, this was something more than that. I couldn't understand how all my training and experience brought me to a school on an Indian reservation in the middle of nowhere with a principal shaking his head at me.

CHAPTER NINETEEN

DEAD END

That night I laid on the couch, eyes wide open and just stared at the ceiling. Where did I go wrong? I thought as far back as my first year teaching, a difficult one for sure, but the first year of teaching is always difficult.

I taught high school for two years and then middle school for two years and I was done. I felt like I had experienced all that teaching had to offer. I wasn't satisfied, so I quit teaching and got a job working in a law office. That was boring. My boss thought that I should consider law school, but then I got the opportunity of a lifetime. I was offered a teaching position at an international school in Sao Paulo, Brazil, so I went back into teaching and I loved it! The students were smart; some were fluent in three languages. The teachers I worked with were creative, talented, and adventurous. I traveled extensively in Brazil and throughout South America. During the summer I started a Master's Degree program in Educational Theatre at New York University. I even got married.

After three years of teaching and traveling throughout South America, my husband and I headed to the South Pacific where I taught at a tiny mission school on the island of American Samoa. My students were eager to learn. We performed plays, entered singing competitions, produced a poetry festival, and got write-ups in the newspaper. It was a glorious time for me in education.

Returning to the United States, I taught at Notre Dame High School while I finished my Master's Degree at New York University. Notre Dame High School was a topflight high school and I was happy they hired me, but after three years I felt had accomplished all I was meant to accomplish in education. One day as I was walking across the campus it dawned on me — everyone else was making money and all I was doing was teaching.

I quit teaching again and on a whim I applied for a job at Paine-Webber, the investment firm. I started my career in finance in 1999 and then the stock market crashed in 2000. My luck. I stuck with it though and I developed an organizational skill set that I hadn't acquired during my years in the classroom. But after seven years of high finance and the rollercoaster ride of the stock market, I was left unfulfilled.

It was late August and on a fluke I picked up the *Los Angeles Times* and looked in the classified ads under "teaching." (People still found jobs in the want ads. The internet hadn't taken off yet, or it was just about to.) And there it was — my dream job: SOCIAL STUDIES/DRAMA. Full-time. Experienced required. Advanced degree preferred. I was so excited about going back into teaching. I had seen what the business world had to offer and the grass wasn't all that greener on the other side. I wanted to go back into the classroom, but now I would bring my organizational skills with me and take my teaching to a whole new level. I typed up my resume and faxed it over.

The next day the vice-principal called me for an interview and I got the job. I was so excited and enthusiastic about being back in the classroom I could hardly contain myself, but my happiness was short-lived. At the end of the year, they did not renew my contract. The principal told me, "You don't fit." I was devastated. This was my dream job. How could this happen?

I got another job at Daniel Murphy Catholic High School, an all-boys Catholic high school in the inner city. I was there for one month when the archdiocese announced that they had decided to close the school down at the end of the school year. I couldn't believe it! All I wanted to do was teach and at the last two schools I worked at, my teaching ended before it barely took off.

Luckily, I got hired at Santa Maria de las Rosas High School. That was going to be it for me, my last stop. The school had a good enrollment, it was close to my house, and the workload was easy. I planned to stay there until I retired. I was prepared for class every day. I never missed a meeting. At the end of two years, I was told that my contract wouldn't be renewed because I didn't know how to teach. With the unemployment rate sky-high, the only teaching job I could find was on an Indian reservation in the middle of nowhere. And now, I couldn't seem to do anything right and all the principal had to say to me was, "I just shake my head at you."

So this is where it all led to? All my education, my training, my hard work, my years of experience, it all led to this? Living on an Indian reservation in the middle of nowhere on a cul-de-sac, literally a dead end. This is where my life took me?

I wanted to go into the principal's office and say, "You shake your head at me because I missed a couple of stage three meetings? Really? Here's something to really shake your head at. I was in education for fifteen years and then I cashed it all in for the business world, which left me dissatisfied and unfulfilled, so I came back into education with enthusiasm and passion and every principal I have ever worked for in the past five years has killed it. They killed my passion and now you shake your head at me because I missed a couple of meetings! Don't shake your head at me because of that, shake your head at me because I've got to be the biggest fool in the world. No matter how many times I get canned, I still want to teach! Go ahead shake your head at that." That's what I wanted to say to the principal. But instead I went to somebody even higher up. That night I went home and had a serious conversation with you know who.

I was lying on my couch and looking up at the ceiling. "Why God? Why? Why does this keep happening to me? No matter where I go, I can't seem to please anybody. 'You don't fit.' 'You don't know how to teach.' 'We are not going to give you a contract.' Now the principal is shaking his head at me? I'm a good teacher. Why does this keep happening to me?"

Nothing. No answer. I tossed and turned. No answer. Only silence. I waited. There was nothing. I would go over it again and again and ask, "Why God? Why? Why does this keep happening to me?" I couldn't understand it. I never had this problem earlier in my career, now when I had the most to offer, no one wanted me. It didn't make any sense. "Why God? Why? Why couldn't I find a school where I could fit in?" 1:00 a.m., 2:00 a.m. No answer. "Why, God? Why? Why does this keep happening to me?" And then I would wait. No answer. And then I would cry out, "Why, God? Why? Why do you keep on calling me to places that don't want me?" And then I would wait. No answer. 3:00 a.m., 4:00 a.m. "You're running out of time, God." I waited and waited. I got no sleep. It had been my longest night ever. And then I gave up. My prayers ceased as I finally accepted the fact that God didn't care. And then, a sliver of light streamed through my blinds. I squinted. And then I heard it. It was as clear as day. "It doesn't matter. It doesn't matter what anyone thinks of your teaching. I've called you to teach, now teach."

I sprung off the couch. "Hey, God! That's a good answer!" Why didn't I think of that? What do I care what the principal thinks? Or the priest? Or the superintendent? God Almighty called me to teach!

I went into the bathroom and looked at myself in the mirror. I looked exactly how I felt — exhausted. My eyes were red and puffy from crying. I had dark circles under them because I hadn't slept all night. I thought about putting on some make-up and then I looked at myself in the mirror and said, "I'm not even going to put on any make-up. All I am going to do today is teach." Besides, I looked so bad no amount of make-up would have made a difference anyway. I showered, got dressed, pulled my hair back in a ponytail and headed off to school.

I walked to school that day empowered, emboldened. God called me to teach. Never again would I allow someone to tear me down or make me feel like I wasn't worthy. I felt like I had been dealt the final blow, but it wouldn't keep me from teaching. So what that I hadn't slept all night and I had dark circles under my eyes. So what that my eyes were all red and puffy from crying. So what that I didn't have any make-up on. None of it mattered because all I was going to do that day was teach. As I crossed the campus and walked towards my classroom I saw Ken. He yelled over to me, "Hey, Luella, don't forget, today's picture day."

CHAPTER TWENTY

PICTURE DAY

Picture day? No! It can't be picture day today. Nobody said anything about today being picture day! I can't get my picture taken today. I have never looked worse in my entire professional career. No that can't be right. As Ken walked across the courtyard, he must have read my mind, because he turned around and said, "Yeah, Luella, don't forget you have to get your picture taken today for the yearbook."

Oh, c'mon! This is ridiculous. I left California, my home, my friends. I put everything in a U-Haul and came up to Montana to teach on an Indian reservation. I forgave the priest who got me fired. And now I have to get my picture taken looking like this? I'm not doing it. I had lost my dignity a long time ago, but I still had my vanity.

What about the principal? He sends out all these stupid emails about stage three meetings, but he doesn't send out an email for picture day? I'm not doing it. They can put "photo not available" next to my name.

I walked over to my classroom adamant about not getting my picture taken, but I somehow knew that by the end of the day, I would go over and get my picture taken and I had no idea how God was going to get me to do it because I wasn't doing it.

I had about ten minutes before the kids would start piling in, so I had a little bit of quiet time to myself. I sat at my desk, organized some papers and then all of a sudden a picture of Saint Sebastian flashed into my mind. It's the one where he is tied to a tree with arrows sticking out of him. 'What am I thinking about him for? First century saint shot with arrows? What does he have to do with anything?' I put it out of my mind and went back to the stack of papers on my desk. A few minutes later an image of Saint Cecelia popped into my head. I hadn't thought of her in years.

When I was in college I used to go to Saint Cecelia's Church in Boston. So you're probably thinking that I was a really good Catholic when I was in college, but I wasn't. Whenever I walked from downtown to my place in Kenmore Square I used to stop at Saint Cecelia's Church just to get out of the cold. Most Catholic churches back East have a main church for weddings, funerals, baptisms, and masses, but then there is a lower basement church that is open during the week. Saint Cecelia's basement, on any given day, was usually filled with a few homeless people, a couple of drunks, one or two die-hard Catholics saying the rosary, and me trying to warm up. At the front of the church under the altar there was a life-size statue of Saint Cecelia lying on her side, decapitated. It had to have been at least thirty years since I had seen that statue. Now all of sudden it was flashing before me.

Why was I thinking about her now? I put it out of my head and then a minute later a picture of Saint Rita popped up. What does she have to do with anything? Saint Rita prayed to share in Christ's sufferings and as the story goes, God gave her a thorn in the middle of her forehead so she could experience the crown of thorns. She walked around for years with that bloodstain in the middle of her forehead and that is how she is depicted on holy cards. What woman wants to be remembered that way?

And then it dawned on me. This is something that is truly unique in the Catholic Church. No other religion does this. Only Catholics do this. We take people at their worst moment; the moment of pain, the moment of suffering, the moment of agony, and we make holy cards ... statues ... calendars... bracelets ... and then we sell them in the gift shop. Well, that's fine for the saints, but I'm no saint and I'm not doing it. I'm not getting my picture taken looking like this.

Then I thought of Saint Bartholomew. When I was in the fifth grade Sister Thomas told us the story of Saint Bartholomew, one of the original twelve apostles. His death was a gory one — skinned alive. Michelangelo painted his picture in the Sistine Chapel. Sister Thomas told us that when we got older we could go to the Sistine Chapel and see it for ourselves.

Twenty years later when I was traveling in Rome the only thing I really wanted to do was to go to the Sistine Chapel and see Michelangelo's rendition of Saint Bartholomew skinned alive. The Sistine Chapel was grandiose, opulent, extravagantly filled with both gory and glorious scenes from the Bible and the lives of the saints. I scanned the entire ceiling and then I found it! Sometimes ceilings do have the answers. There it was. Saint Bartholomew skinned alive. That scene was so vivid, it never left my memory. Now I admit, I looked pretty bad, but I didn't look that bad. So I thought, if Saint Bartholomew was depicted skinned alive for all posterity, I guess I could get my picture taken for the yearbook. I went into the auditorium and got my picture taken. I looked awful, but now I had my very own "holy card."

This was the day that all I was going to do was teach, remember? I didn't get any teaching done at all. The girls were busy fixing their hair and putting on their make-up and the boys were busy watching them fix their hair and put on their make-up. No one was paying any attention to anything I said. I was constantly interrupted by the announcements over the PA: "Seniors whose names begin with A through M report to the auditorium." Some of my students would leave and then about fifteen minutes later they would trickle back to class and then there would be another announcement: "Seniors whose names begin with N through S report to the auditorium." And then they would trickle back to class. "Seniors whose names begin with T through Z report to the auditorium." They would trickle back and then it would start all over again with Juniors, Sophomores, and lastly, Freshmen. And that went on all morning.

By the time lunch rolled around, I was exhausted. I had been up all night waiting for God to get back to me. Living in eternity, He has no sense of time. I didn't know how I was going to get through the next four hours. On top of that, I didn't cover the material I was supposed to with my morning classes and I didn't want my afternoon classes to be ahead of my morning classes, so I couldn't cover any new material. I had to come up with something that would keep them occupied for the rest of the day and keep me awake.

I went over to the art room and frantically searched the shelves and cabinets looking for something, anything that would keep my students busy for the rest of the day. Nothing. I went back into my classroom and frantically looked at the clock. 'Think! Think! You're a creative person! Think of something. You've got four minutes to come up with a lesson plan for the next four hours.' And then… I got it! I got it!

The students rolled in and took their seats, and I made my announcement. "Since today was picture day and I didn't get done with my morning classes what I wanted to get done, and I don't want your classes to be ahead of them, I have a special treat for you. Today we are going to go outside over to the little plaque to Saint Rose of Lima that's right in front of the dorms and we are going to stop and say a prayer. Then we are going to go over to the chapel and say a prayer. Then we are going to walk over to the statue of Blessed Kateri[3] that's in front of the gymnasium and say another prayer … today we are going on a pilgrimage."

One of my students shouted out, "Ms. Wagner, we're not Pilgrims. … we're Indians."

The last thing I needed was for them to go home and tell their parents that I was making them pretend to be pilgrims. "No, not that kind of pilgrim. You're thinking of the Mayflower pilgrims. This is more like a person who travels to different places in search of meaning." For me, I was just trying to stay awake.

For them, they all got really interested in going on a pilgrimage.

"Ms. Wagner there is a replica of the original schoolhouse in the back near the Tongue River, we can go there too," said one student.

"Yeah, there is a grotto to Mother Mary behind the school on the bank of the Tongue River. We can stop there too," said another.

"Okay," I said. "We will visit the schoolhouse and the grotto."

The students were right. There was a log cabin located in the back of the school right next to the Tongue River. It was an exact replica of the original school house. We lucked out. Just as we made our way to the cabin, one of the maintenance crew saw us and asked what we were doing. When I told him we were on a pilgrimage, he offered to open up the cabin and show us the interior. One of the teachers told me that had never been done, so it was a new thing for the students. It was a bit musty, but it was authentic. The cabin housed three rooms; one was a classroom, one was a chapel, and one was the living quarters for the nuns. I just couldn't imagine living on the Tongue River in the middle of the winter without a heater, but I guess those nuns were hard core. I was thankful that my house and my classrooms at least had heaters. Next to the log cabin was a grotto to Mother Mary.

That afternoon I went on three pilgrimages. By the end of the day I was exhausted. I went home and crashed.

CHAPTER TWENTY-ONE

PEACE PIPE

A few days later, I received an email to go to the principal's office immediately after school. 'Now, what?' I thought. All day I was wondering what I had done wrong. Remember, it's never good when you get called to the principal's office. As soon as the last student left my classroom, I headed over to the administration building and waited patiently outside his office. A few minutes later, he called me in and asked me to take a seat. His first comment to me was, "You're off to a rocky start."

I really didn't appreciate the comment. I thought I was doing pretty good. I really thought I would get along with this principal, but why would things be any different on a reservation? He proceeded to tell me, "Yesterday, you didn't take the attendance accurately for your 4th period class."

You have got to be kidding me! This was my nineteenth year teaching, I know how to take attendance. I finally stood up for myself, "No, that's not correct. I did take the attendance accurately."

"No, you didn't."

"Yes, I did."

"You have Levi marked absent, yet he was present."

To which I replied, "That's not correct. Yesterday, when I took the attendance at the beginning of class, Levi was not there. But the other students told me he was in school, that he was just late. Since Levi was not in class at the time of attendance, I marked him absent. I called the attendance office and I explained the situation to your assistant. She told me that if Levi showed up to call the office and I did. I also changed his absence in the computer to a tardy, so I did take the attendance."

He called his assistant into his office and she backed me up 100%. "Yes, Luella called the office to say Levi was not in class. I told her that if he came later she should mark him tardy."

If she hadn't backed me up, he was going to write me up! I saw the pink slip right on his desk. I wanted to seize the moment and say, "See! I did take the attendance! Why don't you just get the hell off my back and let me teach my classes and stop trying to pick a goddamn fight with me over nothing." But instead, I said nothing.

His response was, "Oh, you might have taken the attendance, but it didn't register in the computer. Did you remember to press the green button? Here let me show you how to press the green button."

At that point, I wanted to smack his face, but instead I used the opportunity to practice patience. I told him that next time I would press the green button extra hard when taking the attendance.

The next week, I got what every teacher loves to get. I went to my teacher mailbox and there was the dreaded evaluation form. Attached to the form was a handwritten note from the principal. It read:

Ms. Wagner,

When will be a good time for me to come into your classroom for an observation?

My immediate reaction was, 'Never. I never want you in my classroom.' I felt like walking into his office and saying, "Hey look, why don't we do this. I have a contract for one year. I'll keep my contract till the end of the year and then I'll go. Just stay away from me for the rest of the year. Okay?" That's what I really wanted to do. But I knew that would never work. Besides, it really didn't matter what he thought of me. For the past five years, I had been knocked down so many times by administrators that it just didn't matter anymore. At this stage in my godforsaken career I really didn't care what anyone thought of me.

That night I went home and watched *Shawshank Redemption* for the umpteenth time. One of my favorite scenes is when Red comes up for parole after forty years of incarceration. He has this one great line where he says to the parole officer, "So you go on and stamp your forms, sonny, and stop wasting my time because to tell you the truth, I don't give a shit." I knew exactly how he felt. Those stupid teacher evaluations were just a waste of time and I really didn't give a shit. All I could do was go through the motions and hope for the best, but I really didn't care one way or the other.

I decided to get it over with early in the day. I told my 1st period class, my tenth graders, that the principal was going to be coming in to do an evaluation. I told them, "It's not about you, it's about me and my teaching methodologies, my strategies, my classroom management. And I don't want there to be any surprises. So since we are studying the Old Testament, I was thinking we could dramatize the creation story because it brings together Native American spirituality, the connection with the Creator, nature, animals, and the messages they have for us. It's perfect." Plus, I thought it would give me the opportunity to demonstrate what I had learned from my Master's Degree program at NYU and how I use drama as a methodology.

"Okay who wants to be God?" Nobody wanted to be God. "Look, all you have to do is turn the lights on and off."

Wyatt, very unenthusiastically stood up and said, "Okay, I'll do it."

"Thank you, Wyatt. If you could just take your place over there near the light switch. And can you just turn the lights on and off?"

There was no response. "Wyatt, can you turn the lights on and off, please?" The lights went off. I waited. "Okay, can you turn them back on?" The lights went back on.

Then I asked, "Who wants to be the narrator?" Nobody wanted to be the narrator. "Look, all you have to do is read, that's it."

Jeff took the part, "Okay, I'll do it."

"Okay, Jeff, thank you for your enthusiasm." I was trying to stay positive. "Day two, the waters separated, so why don't we just separate? This side of the classroom can move to this side of the room and the rest of you can move to the other side of the room. C'mon, c'mon, get up out of your chairs."

As students dispersed themselves to opposite sides of the classroom I overheard one of them say, "This is stupid."

I couldn't let that slide. "No, it's not stupid. It's a new way to learn. It's something that you have never done before, but it's not stupid... Okay, day three is vegetation. So, why don't we pretend like we are trees." I demonstrated by waving my hands in the air. "Look we can move like this, like trees blowing in the wind. That's all you have to do. C'mon, it's like a PE class."

"This is so dumb," was the comment from another student.

"No, it's not dumb. Okay, day four, the sun and the moon and the stars. Okay, Ava, could you just stand here? You're going to be the moon." She stood there. "And Michael, could you just stand here? You're going to be the sun." Michael went along with it. "And then the rest of us can stand still, raise our hands and just stretch our fingers in and out like blinking stars. That's all you have to do, just stretch your fingers in and out." They just stared at me.

"Okay, day five — birds and fish. You can decide if you want to be a bird or a fish. And you can make a flying motion or a swimming motion."

"We're not doing that," I heard from another student.

I countered, "No, this is really fun. I used to do this type of thing with my students all the time and they loved it. Really, it's not stupid. C'mon just one more action. All you have to do is be animals and then we have Adam and Eve in the center and then God rests."

They rolled their eyes. It was a lost cause. I gave up.

That night I went home and I said to my cats, "Tiger, Juanita, Moo Moo, I am going to get fired again, and I don't even care this time because it wasn't my idea to begin with."

That night was a restless one. I tossed and turned all night. I woke up tired and groggy, not wanting to face the day. I dragged myself out of bed, got dressed, and I walked to school as though I was walking the gangplank. When I got to my classroom, the principal was already sitting in the back of the room. The kids strolled in. I took the attendance. At least I would get some points for that. I went to the front of the class and said somberly, "Today we are going to reenact the creation story."

I was skeptical as to what would happen next and then miraculously God took his place, the lights went on and off. The narrator got up from his desk and read from the Book of Genesis. The entire creation story unfolded right before my eyes. The students took their cues for each and every action and perfectly demonstrated drama as a methodology. I didn't think they had it in them, yet they did! It was unbelievable! It was as if they had been practicing for weeks.

I sat in the front of the room and didn't budge. I told myself, "Don't move! If you move you'll mess things up." I kept my mouth shut the entire time.

After the creation story, I had the students do a couple more activities and it went flawlessly. The bell rang for the end of class and it was over. When the students left my classroom I was still in a state of shock as to what just happened. The principal got up from his chair in the back of the room and slowly came towards me. I was bewildered as to what his reaction would be. As he approached my desk he looked at me and said, "Wow, those kids really respect you."

I could have said, "Yeah, they're like that all the time. I have them eating out of the palm of my hand every single day." But I had been reading Gandhi's *An Autobiography — The Story of My Experiments with Truth*, the 500-page book that sat on my coffee table for years. Now on the reservation I finally had time to read it. It made an impression because I really wanted to speak the truth, know the truth, and get as close to the truth as possible. When the principal said, "Those students really respect you," I had to be truthful.

"No they don't. They only behaved like that because you were sitting in the back of the room. They never act like that and they will never act like that again."

He chuckled. "Kids are always going to act differently when the principal is in the back of the room."

"I know that."

"You're new on the reservation and these kids are going to test you."

"I know that, too."

"Let me tell you something that you don't know about our kids. When they don't respect the teacher, the teacher says take out a pen and it takes them about ten minutes to get out a pen. Or the teacher says take out your book and it takes another ten minutes for them to get their book out. But you… you had them up and moving around, doing all kinds of movements and actions. They were totally engaged in the lesson. They wouldn't have done that if they didn't respect you."

I wasn't going to argue with him. A few days later I got called to the principal's office and remember, it's never good when you get called to the principal's office.

"Ms. Wagner, have a seat."

I took my seat, just like Red in *Shawshank Redemption*. And then the principal gave me a compliment! "You know, I actually bragged about you to another teacher. I was really impressed with your methods. I can tell it's not your first rodeo."

I had never heard that expression before — "it's not your first rodeo" — but I figured that was how they complimented teachers in Montana.

"I know the first couple of weeks, I gave you a hard time. I realize now that you had a lot to adjust to. So I have a little agenda for you so you can write down meetings and such."

I didn't know what to say. I was really lost for words and then I said the obvious, "Why, thank you."

I was starting to like this guy. He said that his role as a principal was to be supportive of teachers. I couldn't believe my ears. He even said that if I had any suggestions or concerns, that I could email him or come into his office and talk with him about it. I sat there not saying a word. I was just trying to take it all in and then it was my turn. I told him that if ever I was not in a meeting, he could always call me or just remind me over the PA. I found it quite refreshing to have a meaningful and productive one-on-one conversation with the principal. It was an equal sharing of ideas to help the school and the students be the best they could be. It was our own little peace pipe ceremony.

I left his office and as I was walking home, still in a daze, I thought I felt the earth move. A hundred years from now astronomers will record an unexplained planetary shift. But you, the reader, will know what caused it. For the past five years I had experienced nothing but a string of thankless administrators and now I finally had a principal who appreciated what I was doing in the classroom and it was such an extraordinary event that even the planets reacted to it.

As soon as I got home I shared the news with my cats, "Tiger! Juanita! Moo Moo! You're never going to believe this, but the principal actually likes what I am doing in the classroom. It's about time." Now what was I going to do? I was honestly looking forward to getting fired this time. And then it sunk in. I was stuck.

CHAPTER TWENTY-TWO

SNOW DAY

By the time Thanksgiving had rolled around it was pretty cold and bitter. I didn't even want to step outside, but the nuns had invited us over for Thanksgiving dinner. Since I was not in the mood to cook, and I am never in the mood to cook, I decided to go. Carole picked me up and we spent the whole day with the nuns. Thank God they had wine. We had a great home-cooked meal, something that I had not had in months, and boy, did it taste good. And so did the wine. That's how I spent my Thanksgiving on the reservation — no Indians, just nuns.

Sister Bernadette had been a real blessing to me, not because she invited me over for Thanksgiving, and not just because she hired me. She helped to restore my faith in Catholic education. After working at so many lackluster Catholic schools that were run on nepotism and ignorance, it was encouraging to know that there was one person in administration who knew what they were doing. Even though we did not talk often, when we did, her words were always inspirational and supportive. She was the mission director and she was well-suited for the position. She had a wealth of knowledge and experience having worked in both schools and hospitals. She had a clear understanding of mission and purpose. When she came to the school, she wrote a new mission statement that was placed prominently in every single classroom. I wasn't aware of it yet, but that single, solitary act would play an important part in my reason for being there.

That night I had a dream about an egg. It was a hard-boiled egg, a deviled egg, cut in half and filled with the yoke and mayo and seasonings. But the egg was huge. It was the biggest egg I had ever seen — like six feet tall. When I woke up the next morning the vision was still vivid in my mind. When I looked up egg in my dream dictionary it said that eggs were symbolic of creativity and inspiration. It also said that an egg symbolizes major transformation.

I thought it might have something to do with sweat lodges and the womb experience. Even though my biological clock had stopped ticking a long time ago, I had to be open to the possibility that something new was happening in my life. Or it might just be that I ate a lot the day before and I was still thinking about food. Whatever the meaning behind it, I took it as a good sign.

The rest of the long weekend was rather peaceful and relaxing. By the time Monday rolled around I didn't feel like going back to school, but with only three weeks before Christmas break, I mustered up what little self-discipline I had, rolled out of bed, and got ready for school. Dressing for Montana included two stages: first, the regular clothes, a pair of pants and a shirt. Then there was the second stage — another pair of pants, a sweater, a jacket, a scarf, gloves, earmuffs, and of course, my boots. Every morning my cats stared at me as I added layer upon layer before leaving and saying "good-bye." For them it was a warning to never even think about going outside.

I opened the door and there in front of me, nature had placed another foot of snow over the already existing snow. While it was beautiful to look at and quietness filled the air, I still had the task of walking through it to get to school. I looked back at my cats, envious of their warm cozy spot, turned and closed the door and began my trek through the foot-high snow. When I reached the end of my driveway, as luck would have it my neighbor pulled up. She worked in the mailroom at school and whenever she saw me walking she always picked me up and gave me a ride. I gleefully opened the car door and hopped in.

"Hey, thanks for always picking me up. Can you believe all this snow? I never saw this much snow even in Massachusetts. You know in Massachusetts we would get snow, but it would melt. Here in Montana it just keeps piling up and it never seems to go away."

"Luella, don't you know?"

"Know what?"

She looked at me concerned, "Luella, didn't anybody call you?"

"No, nobody called me."

"Luella, you don't know?"

"Know what?"

"Luella, there's no school today, it's a snow day."

"A snow day! That's the best thing I've heard since I got here. But why are you going to work?"

"Luella, I work in the mailroom, nothing stops us."

I got out of her car and jumped up and down back to my house waving my hands up at the sky in total bliss. What a great day! A snow day! My first snow day as a teacher! I had that little kid feeling all over again.

When you're a little kid and you go to Disneyland it is a great feeling, but when you go back as an adult it just isn't the same. The same is true of Christmas. When you're a little kid, opening up all the presents under the tree at Christmas time is a great feeling, but when you get older it just isn't the same. As an adult it's rare to ever experience those little kid feelings again. I remember that time in second grade when my mother woke me up and said, "Look out the window," and there outside my bedroom window were mounds of snow covering the back yard. And then she said, "There's no school today!" I still remember that happy little kid feeling, but as a teacher, it's ten times better.

I opened the door and my cats looked at me as if to say, "Why are you back so soon?"

"It's a snow day!" I told them.

They went back to sleep while I tossed off all my layers of winter wardrobe and turned up the heat full blast. So now what was I going to do?

'I know, I'll write out some Christmas cards,' I thought.

I love sending out Christmas cards. Every year I sent out Christmas cards that were a reflection of where I was in life. Like the time I went to Tahiti for the holidays, my card was an illustration of a palm tree decorated with Christmas lights gracing the beach. For this year, I was a bit more spiritual and chose a card with a Native American nativity scene on the front and a Native American blessing inside. I thought it was so appropriate for this time in my life: "From my home on the reservation to yours — wishing you a peaceful Christmas and joyous New Year."

I pulled out my Christmas card list of names and addresses from the previous year and started writing. I came across the name and address of a very good friend of mine who I hadn't spoken to in quite a while. He didn't even know I was in Montana. I had met Paul years ago on an Alaskan cruise — the one you normally do in your eighties, I did in my forties. We remained friends ever since. He was from Long Beach and since we didn't live that far from one another we occasionally met for lunch or dinner. He reminded me of the Nick Nolte character in *Peaceful Warrior*. He was a very kind man; a bit of a father figure.

I decided to give him a call. Even though it had been a while we picked up right where we left off. It was as if no time had passed between us.

The phone rang. "Hello."

"Paul, it's Luella."

"Hey, Lu, I haven't heard from you in a long time. Where have you been?"

"Well, you're never going to believe this. I'm living in Montana."

"Montana!"

"Yes, Montana. I'm teaching high school on an Indian reservation."

"An Indian reservation? How did that happen?"

"Oh, Paul, it was so unjust. I didn't do anything wrong and this priest got me fired from my last job and this was the only job I could find in the entire country."

"So, what are you doing up there?"

"Oh, what am I doing up here?" I wanted to put a positive spin on things so I told him about all the cultural events I was involved in. "Oh, Paul, I've gone to powwows, sweat lodges, healing ceremonies. I am taking a class at Chief Dull Knife Community College on the History of the Cheyenne People. I went on a field trip to the Battle of Little Bighorn. I went to Sheridan, Wyoming where Buffalo Bill held his auditions for his Wild West Show. And next semester I am going to take a beadwork class at the Beadwork Institute. I am going to learn how to do beadwork."

"Luella, that sounds wonderful, but what are you doing for those kids?"

"What am I doing for those kids? You've got to be kidding me! I came fifteen hundred miles in a U-Haul to teach these kids religion. That's what I am doing for these kids."

"Anybody can do that."

"WHAT!!!!!"

"Anybody can do what you did. That's no big deal."

I was shocked. "What are you talking about?"

"Luella, I know you are upset about being fired, but that has nothing to do with you being on the reservation."

"Of course, it does. I was fired unjustly and this was the only school in the country that wanted me."

"Luella, that's not the reason why you're there. You're there because your soul called you to that reservation to do something special for those kids and you're going to be there as long as it takes for you to find out what it is and then do it."

Up until that point, I didn't really know why I was called to the reservation. For the longest time I thought I was being punished and I didn't even know what I did wrong. The job did provide me with a stable income and I was able to pay my bills, but I never even considered doing something "special" for those kids. They were the toughest bunch of kids I had ever taught. I was reminded again of *Peaceful Warrior*. It was a line that went "Those that are the hardest to love are the ones that need it the most." And then I thought, 'If I am supposed to do something special for these kids, I better figure it out soon, because I can't take another one of these Montana winters.'

CHAPTER TWENTY-THREE

CHRISTMAS ON THE REZ

The school was producing their annual Christmas musical and I had no intention of going until one of my students from my 7th period class, said to me, "Hey, Ms. Wagner, since you're practically my grandmother, can you come to see me in the Christmas play tonight? I want to be able to look out into the audience and see someone I know."

I laughed and thought, 'Grandmother! I must really be looking old to these kids!' But I took it as a compliment, since grandparents are revered in Native American culture. I also felt bad that no one else was going to be there for her. I didn't know what her family situation was and I didn't ask. I decided to go to the Christmas musical and support her. She would look out from the stage and see me there.

When I got to the auditorium that night, I found a seat next to Ed, the math teacher and his wife. Ed was an excellent math teacher. There is something special about math teachers. They know how to solve problems and they teach other people how to solve problems. The one thing you get in life is problems. There is no debate about the answer in math. It is either right or wrong; there is no opinion. Math teachers teach you how to find the truth. That's why it is always good to know a math teacher. I was happy to know Ed.

Ed had been a missionary in the Philippines which is where he met his wife. They came back to the United States and Ed could have taught anywhere in the world, yet he chose the reservation. He found his niche. I was still looking for mine. That night as we sat waiting for the curtain to come up, he asked me where I was going for the holidays. When I told him I was staying on the reservation he said, a bit surprised, "You're not leaving?"

"No, I'm not. I'm staying here the whole time, but I do have a friend visiting."

He was impressed with my determination to stick it out and not go home. It really wasn't determination, it was more financial than anything else. I just couldn't afford to go home. The curtain came up and there was "my granddaughter" and I made sure she saw me. After the show, she totally ignored me.

The next week, we had our faculty Christmas party — 7:00 p.m. in the school dining hall on a Saturday night. I got a ride to and from the school, so I didn't have to worry about walking in the cold and freezing to death.

The dining hall was packed. I had never seen it so crowded before. It was quite a lavish Christmas party with the exception of one thing. There was no alcohol, not a drop. Water, that was the only beverage served. It was encouraging to see that adults can have a good time without any alcohol. While everyone was celebrating the holidays, I was celebrating something else. I was beginning to see the transformation that was taking place in my life. Since coming to the reservation, I had done extensive reading and writing. I had learned about the history of the area. I had visited battle sites and sacred sites. I had gone to sweat lodge ceremonies and healing ceremonies, but most importantly, I was learning about myself, what I could endure and what I was capable of. Yes, it was a cause for celebration. I had no clue that the toughest part was yet to come.

I was so excited about Christmas break, I couldn't even teach. The last few days of school we watched *The Polar Express* with Tom Hanks. Once school got out I was looking at two weeks of vacation time and boy, did I need it. The other teacher from California invited me over to her house for lunch on Christmas Day. I went over early in the afternoon. We watched TV and had a chance to talk. She worked in the lower school, so we didn't see each other as much. When we did, we took full advantage of it. She was a great cook too. She knew I was a vegetarian so she made cheese enchiladas with a plate of beans on the side.

Another teacher had invited us over to her house for Christmas dinner. She worked in the middle school so I didn't see her a lot either, but she stands out in my mind even to this day. The first week of school, I was in the cafeteria lunch line when she approached me and asked me if I had a lunch ticket and when I told her I didn't, she gave me hers. That same welcoming teacher invited my friend and me over to her house for Christmas dinner with her entire family.

We drove over, got out of the car, walked through the knee-deep snow, knocked on the door, and as soon as the door opened it hit me. It was an intense smell of cooked "something." I couldn't really identify what it was, but it was a really strong, pungent smell. I had been living on bagels and cream cheese, Rice Krispy bars, and frozen pizza for months — the smell of cooked "something" was so intense it was making me gag. I didn't know what they were cooking and I didn't want to know, but I think it was some kind of meat. I didn't judge either. I was reading Gandhi, who said that if you judged a person for eating meat, it was worse than eating meat.

I wanted to step outside for a breath of fresh air, but I couldn't because the temperature was below zero. I had to adapt to the situation. If I took short little breaths the smell didn't seem to be as strong, or I could breathe through my mouth. It was somewhat of a remedy, but the smell was still there. The thing that saved me was the crucifix that hung on the wall in the dining room. I had something to focus on, so every time I inhaled I stared at the cross and it didn't smell so bad. As the food was being prepared I made small talk with the person sitting next to me, while I tried to think of how I was going to get around that fact that I was a vegetarian. They were so kind to invite me to their home for Christmas dinner, yet I didn't want to offend them by not eating whatever it was they were serving.

Then it was time for us to all have dinner and that's when my friend announced, "Luella's a vegetarian." Everybody got quiet.

I thought, 'How am I going to explain this? They will never understand.'

And then I experienced true Montana hospitality, "Oh Luella, we didn't know you were a vegetarian. We have a whole selection of vegetables on this table. And we have more vegetables in the refrigerator." People were tripping over themselves to get me a full plate of vegetables. I had plenty to eat and we all had a memorable Christmas. And a funny thing happened. Once I started eating, the smell, whatever it was, didn't bother me anymore.

CHAPTER TWENTY-FOUR

CABIN FEVER

The next day, I picked up Marian up at the airport. I had gotten a ride to Billings a few days before and rented a car. It was hard to imagine that I hadn't driven a car in almost four months. In California, you can't live without one. Here on the reservation, it was liberating not to have one.

How can I describe Marian? She was a teacher friend of mine I had known for years. I met her my first year of teaching and no matter where I went she always followed me, so naturally she followed me to the reservation. She was an anomaly, a bit of a busybody with her own quirky style. It had been seven months since I had last seen her when we celebrated Mother's Day and I told her that I planned on staying at Santa Maria de las Rosas High School. A lot had happened since then.

When I got to the airport, Marian's flight had been delayed, but I enjoyed the wait. It gave me the opportunity to "people watch." Finally, Marian came down the escalator. She wasn't hard to miss. She stood head and shoulders above everyone else. Her clothes were suited for the climate, but the big oversized curly red wig just didn't fit the Montana scene and I didn't have the courage to tell her that she looked a bit out of place. For the past few years, Marian had adopted wigs as part of her fashion statement. She suffered from hair loss and like any other woman, she wanted hair. I know that feeling. Like when I couldn't let go of my hair extensions and I tied them together in a ponytail and wore them that way to school every day. Marian was the same way, she couldn't let go of her big red wigs, even if they didn't fit her face. If she looked in the mirror and liked what she saw, so be it. She was only going to be here for a few days and it wasn't worth losing a friendship over.

Before we headed back to the reservation, I made a quick stop at Walmart for some groceries and a couple of bottles of wine. I knew I would need them. As we were walking out of Walmart, Marian pointed to the hair salon and said, "Honey, look, you can get your hair done here." I guess that was her subtle way of letting me know that my hair looked like crap. I thought it was a bit ironic, considering she was walking around with a red mop on her head. I shrugged it off.

Yes, I knew that my hair looked like crap, but I just wasn't going to take a chance and have it done at Walmart. There were too many times when I put my hair in the hands of a total stranger and ended up with chopped hair, crooked bangs, and I will never forget the hair "stylist" who cut my ear! Call it pride or call it vanity, but I was used to Gail at Casablanca Hair Salon in Sherman Oaks. If I couldn't have it done there I wasn't going to have it done at all. My homemade ponytail extensions would suffice.

I have to admit it. I didn't have the best accommodations for Marian. While Marian was sleeping on the blow-up bed that Eufemia gave me, it sprung a leak. I told her I was sorry and that I would spend the next few nights on the floor and she could have the couch.

The first day of Marian's visit, we visited the Amish store and I introduced her to Rebecca. It was daylight, so we could see all that the store had to offer. Marian was expecting a showroom of bed frames, couches, rocking chairs and such, not shelves of dented cans and expired salad dressings, but that was the reality.

We came back to school and I showed her the Northern Cheyenne Indian Museum and then I took her over to my classroom. That night I tried to explain to her the challenges I was up against, but the conversation only made things worse. Marian's remedy was, "Honey, don't you think you would feel better if you only had a man in your life?" Like that was the answer to life's problems. I had been married once and for me, I enjoyed the single life. I really didn't want or need a man in my life at that time. It would just have made things even more complicated. The conversation was over.

The next day was beautiful. The village was steeped in snow, but the sun was out, the roads were clear, and it was a good day for travel. I wanted to go to Bear Butte State Park. Parts of the park were sacred to Native Americans. I thought it would be a nice place to end the year and begin the new one. Marian wanted to go to Mount Rushmore, not exactly a sacred spot for Natives. We decided on Bear Butte, and then we would play it by ear. I was following the map exactly when we came to a fork in the road. I wanted to go the scenic route, but Marian insisted that we didn't have time and we should take the highway. All the way I was looking for Route 385. After about thirty minutes I came to a stop. I got out the map. I didn't have an iPhone, so no Waze or Google maps. Even if I did, I don't know how good the coverage would have been in those parts, so I was relying on the old fashioned way of getting somewhere.

I took a look at the map and realized that we should have taken the scenic route after all. By taking the highway we went right past Bear Butte and were headed for Mount Rushmore. Marian ended up getting her way after all. Once we got there, the place was a ghost town. It was a tourist spot in the summer, but since it was winter, the place was deserted. Well, there were some people there, but very few. We stopped at one of the jewelry stores and I got a pair of Black Hills gold earrings. I have always wanted Black Hills gold, ever since a waitress I worked with at the Hilton Hotel in Burbank had mentioned it to me over twenty-five years ago.

It was still light out and we were able to take the scenic route back. We passed through Deadwood, named after the dead trees that the early settlers found there. With the discovery of gold in the Black Hills in 1874 it became a boom town. The town was filled with Wild Wild West history. Among its inhabitants were Wild Bill Hickok and Calamity Jane, who are also buried there. I wanted to make at least a stop and check out the saloons and casinos, but Marian wasn't in the mood. So I kept driving and then Marian got hungry so we stopped for dinner at Spearfish, a small town located on the border of South Dakota and Montana. We didn't have much of a conversation. I was still pissed about taking the wrong route and by this time it was too dark to go to Bear Butte.

The next day, Marian wanted to go to Sheridan. I was tired after the eight-hour drive the day before and I just wasn't up to another long drive. She would have to settle for the Battle of Little Bighorn. It was only forty-five minutes away. Once we got there, I showed Marian the spot where Custer had his Last Stand. The place was pretty deserted too. Like Mount Rushmore, no one was around. Well, almost no one. Then a carload of Indians went by hootin' and hollerin' and Marian looked at me and said, "What's that about?"

"Who knows!" I said. But I guessed why they were hootin' and hollerin' — because they probably never saw someone with a big red mop on their head.

After the battle site I walked over to the museum. Even though I was sure it was closed, I tried the door anyway and to my surprise the door opened. Marian and I both went inside and watched a short video about the battle and then I did a little shopping. I bought a couple of books — one on Crazy Horse and another one on Black Elk. Marian did a little souvenir shopping as well and then we headed back to the reservation.

New Year's Eve was swinging. We went out to dinner at the Hitching Post, a tiny café in town. Marian had steak. I had a salad. The Hitching Post closed at 8:00 p.m., so did the rest of the town. We went back to my place and watched *Apollo 13*. Marian said it made her blood pressure go up. The movie ended right about 12:00 midnight and then the family across the street had a little tiny fireworks display to bring in the New Year.

Call it cabin fever or just plain getting on my nerves, but there were so many times when I really wanted to smack her. Like when she was in the kitchen trying to help me cook and she flipped the veggie burgers right after I had done it, or when she opened up the blinds in the kitchen to let the light in when I wanted to keep them closed, or when she told me I needed to get my hair done. All of those things were really irksome, but in a crazy sort of way I was glad that she came up. I had made friends in Montana, but there's nothing like having an old friend to spend the holidays with, even if there are a few irritations thrown in. I didn't have the money to go home and even if I did, I am not sure I would have. I wanted to have the full Montana experience without any interruptions. So I was really glad that Marian came up. I felt like she had helped me over the hump. I had made it this far. I knew I could make it to the end of the school year. December had been the darkest month, now the days would start to get longer, even if only for a minute or two.

CHAPTER TWENTY-FIVE

TEACHER IN THE YELLOW HOUSE

January is one of my favorite months. It's a time of new beginnings. I always anticipate something good happening in January and it generally does. But then again, I always get sick in January and this year was no different. We went back to school the first week of January and that's when I began to feel that first sign of a scratchy throat that you ignore, deny, fight against, but ultimately give into. I was in the copy room coughing uncontrollably, when the office manager said, "Luella, you sound terrible. You really should go to the clinic. I can give you a ride up to the clinic after school, but I can't wait for you. You will have to get a ride back."

"Thanks for the ride up. I can get a ride back. Somebody always picks me up."

Once school got out, she gave me a ride up to the clinic. It was still light out and I didn't think I would be long and I thought for sure I would be able to get a ride back.

As I entered the clinic, it was obvious that I was not the only one who was sick. There were several other people and a couple of kids sitting in the waiting room who were coughing and sneezing like I was. I checked myself in with the receptionist, sat down, leafed through some magazines and waited. And waited. And waited. Finally, after no one else was left, my name was called. The doctor seemed very kind and caring. She took all my vital signs and then told me, "Well, there's nothing I can do for you. It's viral and all you can do is ride it out."

I was so disappointed. "You can't do anything for me?"

"You have the flu and all you can do is just let it run its course. Get some rest and drink plenty of fluids."

"Can't you give me something?"

"There's really nothing I can prescribe for you."

"Not even antibiotics?"

"No, not even antibiotics. Your infection is viral. Antibiotics won't work. You just have to let it run its course."

"What about NyQuil? Can I take that?"

"Yes, you can take NyQuil. That will at least help you to sleep."

As I stepped out of the clinic, the cold air hit my face and the rest of my body braced against the freezing temperatures. It was dark and it was late. The possibility of a car passing by was slim and the chances that someone would see me walking in the dark were even slimmer. I stood there. I hesitated. I was reminded of the story I read in elementary school by Jack London, *To Build a Fire*. It really left an impression because some forty years later I still remembered it. My subconscious mind must have known that someday I was going to have a similar experience. It's the story of a man traveling through the Yukon with his dog. He stopped to build a fire. It took him several tries, but he finally got the match lit. I always remembered the part when a horrific smell flooded his nostrils. It was the smell of his own flesh burning. He was so numb from the cold he couldn't feel that his flesh was on fire. He could only smell it. He never succeeded in building a fire. He collapsed and died in the snow, while his dog made it back to the lodge.

At that moment outside the clinic, I started to think, 'That could happen to me. That could really happen to me.' I imagined myself collapsing in the snow and being buried alive. It wouldn't be until spring when the snow melted that someone would drive by and say, "Hey, there's that teacher, we've been looking for. We thought she went back to Los Angeles. She's been buried under that pile of snow all this time."

But I had to get my NyQuil. So I started walking in the dark, in the snow, in negative-degree temperatures. No one saw me, no one stopped. As I trudged through the snow I had only one thought — 'This is insane!' I kept repeating it over and over again as I walked in freezing cold temperatures with the flu! 'This is insane! This is insane!' This whole time on the reservation, I really thought that I was doing God's will and while I could accept everything that had happened so far, this was total insanity. Then came the moment of truth, 'What kind of god am I following? Who would require such an insane act?' The wind was blowing in my face and with each step my body sank deeper and deeper into the snow. But then I thought, 'There must be a god, who is keeping me going because what I am doing is not humanly possible. How else could I be doing this?' I was on the verge of collapsing, yet I still found the strength to keep walking.

I finally reached the Trading Post. Once I opened the door and stepped inside, the warm air and the fluorescent lights awakened my quasi-lifeless body. I was glad to be out of the cold. And then I had the dreadful thought, 'what if they are out of NyQuil and I made this entire trip for nothing?' It was a small store and they often ran out of things and judging from the clinic there were a lot of people in the village who were sick. I made my way to the medicine shelf and once I spotted the bottles of NyQuil I felt a sense of relief. Just looking at the NyQuil made me feel better. I knew that once I took it, I would fall asleep right away and be out of my misery. I grabbed the bottle of NyQuil and stood in line for the cashier. I still didn't know how I was going to get home.

I felt a tap on my shoulder. "Excuse me, you're the teacher in the yellow house."

I looked at this woman who I had never seen before and said, "Yes, I am."

"I know you don't have a car, and you really shouldn't be walking in this cold weather. Can I give you a ride?"

I was so grateful, but I didn't want her to get what I had. "Are you sure you want to give me a ride? I have the flu."

Without any hesitation she said, "Of course, I will give you a ride home, don't even think for a moment that I wouldn't."

So this woman who I didn't even know ended up saving my life because if it wasn't for her, I would have walked the two miles in the snow and I probably would have collapsed and died like the guy in the Jack London story. I don't know who she was and I never saw her again, but I will always be grateful for the ride back home. She truly was a Good Samaritan.

Once I entered my house, I crashed on the couch and began the most agonizing two weeks of my entire time on the reservation.

NyQuil doesn't work in Montana. I usually conk out right after taking it, but now I was wide awake and the coughing just wouldn't stop. I coughed so much I thought I was going to vomit my esophagus. I was tired, sick, and weak, yet my body still had enough energy to keep on coughing. Even my cats didn't want to be around me. I was glad because I didn't want them to catch whatever it was I had. I called in sick every day for two weeks. I could barely say a sentence without it being interrupted by my coughing. At least when I called in sick they knew I wasn't faking it.

All I could do was lie on the couch and cough and hopefully at some point, get some sleep. When I wasn't sleeping, all I did was lie on my back and think. It was pretty depressing. I was more than sick with a cold, I was sick with my life. My entire career in education didn't amount to much. I had followed God's will and done what I thought He wanted me to do and it all led to this — sick on the couch in a little yellow house on a dead-end street in the middle of nowhere. I had no more energy, no more passion, and I never did find my true purpose. My entire life — what a waste. I turned on the DVD player and watched *Shawshank Redemption* one more time.

After two weeks of lying sick on the couch, I started feeling a little bit better. Even though it was only January, I started packing to go home, still wondering why I had come here in the first place.

One night I peered out the bedroom window. It was dark, not a streetlight in the area, only moonlight. Even the house across the street was shrouded in darkness. It was so quiet; not a sound as nature slept. There was no motion, no activity at all. For some unknown reason this gave me great consolation. I sat there and stared. I stared at the moon. I stared at the cottonwood tree in my front yard. I watched for something to happen, something to move, but there was no motion at all. It was the dead of winter. And I was in the middle of it — the stillness — a force so strong, so pervasive I wondered why it took me so long to find it. As I sat there surrounded by the stillness, I wanted nothing. I desired nothing. I felt no pain, no sorrow. Nothing hurt. Everything in the past was forgotten and the future didn't matter. It was an incredible feeling — to be at peace with myself and the world around me.

There was something very special about that space. For the next couple of nights I would sit and stare out the window and suddenly the world opened up to me. In those dark moments, things began to get bright. That was probably my favorite place on the reservation, sitting in the stillness looking out my bedroom window in the dead of night. It was worth coming to the reservation just for those moments. And then things started to change for me.

CHAPTER TWENTY-SIX

RESERVATION BASKETBALL

They say absence makes the heart grow fonder. It certainly rang true for me, at least on the reservation. I don't know what I did, but once I got over my sickness and returned to school, those kids loved me — well, okay, they liked me a lot. Like the time there was still snow on the ground when I was walking over to my classroom and two of my students were playing basketball on the court and I heard one of them say, "Hey, let's help Ms. Wagner, so she won't fall down."

They both came running over to me and with one on my left and the other on my right, they held onto both my arms, so I wouldn't fall down. I could have walked by myself, but it was so much better with both of them by my side.

"You know we have to help Ms. Wagner, she is getting a little old," said one boy.

"Don't worry Ms. Wagner we'll hold on to you so you won't fall down," said the other.

Oh, if only they were there for me six months before when I was slipping and sliding all over the place.

They walked with me to my classroom and asked if there was anything else they could do for me. I thanked them graciously and told them I would call on them the next time I needed help walking across the campus. Even though the snow still hadn't melted, I finally broke the ice with my students.

Basketball was big on the reservation. What the school lacked on the football field — our football team wasn't very good — we made up for on the basketball court. One day, one of the junior class moderators asked me if I could work the concession stand for the basketball game that night. The concession stand was a fundraiser for the junior class that would pay for their field trip to Seattle in March. Going on the field trip was a requirement for all the junior moderators and I was one of them. Sister Bernadette forgot to mention that during my interview. If she had, it would have been a dealbreaker. I never would have taken a job that required me to go to another state and leave my cats for five days. Luckily for me, one of the Jesuit volunteers offered to go in my place. Since I had bailed on the five-day field trip to Seattle, I was obligated to work the concession stand.

I figured we would sell a couple of hot dogs and that would be it. For the football games there was hardly any business. 'Good luck at raising money for the junior class field trip,' I thought. I went home, took a nap, and headed back to school around 4:45 p.m. I couldn't believe the sight I saw when I got there. The place was crowded and the lines at the concession stand were seven or eight people deep. Teachers and students were already manning the counter and one of them asked, "Why are you late?"

"Sorry, I really didn't think there would be a crowd of people wanting hot dogs and hamburgers." I couldn't believe that there were this many people living in the area and it was even harder to believe that they would leave their warm cozy homes and venture out into freezing cold temperatures just for a high school basketball game. But that's exactly what they did. It was a night out for the entire family.

I hung up my coat, got behind the counter and worked four hours straight taking orders for hot dogs, hamburgers, drinks, cheese nachos, candies, beef jerky, and popcorn. As busy as it was, I did get the chance to sneak away and watch about two minutes of the game. We won. I worked until 9:45 p.m. and then I went home and crashed on the couch.

The team continued their winning streak and made it to the playoffs in Miles City. A majority of the students went with them to show their support. With most of the kids gone, we finished up our lessons early and when one of my students asked if they could work on posters to welcome the players home, I said, "Sure."

Word got out and all of a sudden, students were pouring into my classroom. The door would open and a student would say, "Ms. Wagner, can we work on posters in here too?"

"Of course, as long as it's okay with your teacher." The other teachers were fine with it, since they all had smaller class sizes too that week and the students were able to finish all their work early.

It was starting to look like my classroom again. Students were working together, creating and designing artwork as we all listened to the game on the internet. They were happy and so was I. It was just like the old days when I was at Santa Maria de las Rosas.

And then out of nowhere a student remarked, "Hey, Ms. Wagner, you never cracked."

I looked at him and said, "What? You think I'm on crack?" Everybody started laughing. He looked at me and said, "No! No! You never cracked."

"What do you mean?" I asked.

"You never got angry with us. No matter what we did, you never yelled at us. We see teachers come through here all the time and we wear them down. They start off all happy and then they can't take it and they crack. But you never cracked."

"It's only February," I said. "There's still time." Everyone laughed.

That was one of the best compliments that I had ever gotten as a teacher. One student reminded me, "Remember that time you wanted us to clear our desks and I gave you a really hard time about it?"

"Yes." I thought to myself, 'How could I ever forget?'

And then he remarked, "I couldn't believe it. You didn't get angry with me. No matter what I said, you didn't get mad. You're like my grandmother. You have a lot of patience. You must have taught a lot of kids, huh?"

"Probably a couple thousand," I responded.

My philosophy of education worked. Patience under all circumstances is the key to classroom success. I firmly believe that no matter what subject or what grade a teacher teaches, patience is the virtue that needs to be incorporated at every level. No matter what students do, patience and time will eventually win them over. And that is one of the most valuable lessons that one can teach.

Later, I mentioned it to Ed, the math teacher, and I said, "I know they don't mean it — to intentionally wear a teacher down." He looked at me and said, "Oh yes, they do." And then we both laughed.

Even though my students were beginning to warm up to me, the temperatures were still in the negatives. One night as I was walking home from school, it was so cold I thought my blood would freeze. I pictured myself as one of those wooden Indian constructed cut-outs that you see on the hills and the battlefields in Montana. I told myself that as long as I kept moving, my blood wouldn't freeze. I started to sing *Here Comes the Sun*. I used to sing that a lot. Whether I was walking in the dark going to school or walking in the dark coming home, I would sing *Here Comes the Sun*. It gave me hope and consolation. Right after I started singing that, someone came by in a pickup truck. "Hey, you shouldn't be walking in this weather. Hop in."

Montana is filled with Good Samaritans. I jumped in. He gave me a ride to my house and I thanked him immensely. It's amazing how weather brings out the best in people. While we don't have severe snowstorms in Los Angeles, I have experienced a couple of earthquakes and I have found that in the midst of misery the human spirit comes alive and people's inborn desire to help one another shines through. Each person understands that when they are helping someone through a difficult time it makes the world a better place. It is a great reminder of why we are all here.

CHAPTER TWENTY-SEVEN

BEADWORK

I signed up for a beadwork class through Chief Dull Knife Community College, but it was taught at my school. The instructor was Philippe Franquelin. He was from France. What were the chances of meeting up with a Frenchman on an Indian reservation in southeastern Montana? It was not a random occurrence at all. Philippe was born in Paris and raised in Berry, a region known for fine foods and wine, yet it was his destiny to live and work with Native Americans in Montana.

His older brother, Jean-Pierre, had the biggest influence on his life with a unique collection of Native American memorabilia, yet it was the environment in which Philippe and his brother were raised that shaped their understanding and appreciation of the Native American life. I had long known that the history of the French and Indians in America was vastly different from that of the British. In France, interest in Native American ways dated back to Louis XIV. Interest grew when Buffalo Bill brought over his Wild West Show in the late 1800s. With the invention of cinema and the introduction of the "western" in the early 1900s featuring French actor Joe Hamman, the stage was set for both Jean-Pierre and Philippe's love of and fascination with Native American culture.

While Jean-Pierre dreamed of opening a French restaurant imbued with his collection of American Indian artifacts, Philippe studied Native American history and customs and started learning beadwork. The two brothers came up with a plan. Philippe would go to culinary school and then help Jean-Pierre launch his Native American themed restaurant, but then tragedy struck. Jean-Pierre died unexpectedly. Coping with the death of his brother, Philippe decided to leave France and move to London. He found fulfillment working as a sommelier at the Interlude de Tabaillaud restaurant in Covent Garden, a world-class luxury shopping district with elegant dining and easy access to the theatres in the area. When

Philippe wasn't using his skills and talents in the restaurant, he visited museums, exhibits, and galleries that featured Native American art and artifacts. It was always Philippe's destiny to come to America and work with Natives so when a Cheyenne invited him to Montana it was an easy decision to make. Philippe eventually settled on the Northern Cheyenne Indian reservation where he found a job teaching beadwork and ledger work to the students at the school. He also founded the Beadwork Institute that focuses on teaching the art of beadmaking while promoting Native American tradition.[4] I considered myself fortunate to be one of his students.

Philippe was soft-spoken and kind. He was also very patient — the one characteristic that is essential for beadwork. Beadwork requires so much concentration and it can't be rushed, and to teach beadwork requires even more patience. In addition to being incredibly patient, Philippe was an excellent "hands-on" teacher. Anyone who took Philippe's class became thoroughly engaged in creating their very own unique beadwork masterpiece. Philippe guided the process by explaining the different patterns, symbols, and color combinations found in Native American art. He also created a nurturing, edifying classroom environment. There was something very therapeutic about stepping out into the cold air, walking to school, and then entering a warm classroom, but it was more than just the temperature. It was an energy that encouraged everyone to share their ideas, questions, concerns, whatever it was that they wanted to talk about. It was that kind of classroom.

Philippe was also a fabulous storyteller. He told us the story of a man he knew from South Dakota who lived in tepee for a year. Philippe said that the man was able to get his life back on track by attuning himself with nature. Phillippe often spoke about the importance of connecting with the elements by getting as close to nature as possible. I reminded myself again how fortunate I was to be in Montana and to have the opportunity to immerse myself in nature. I didn't live in a tepee, but I was living in the great outdoors, surrounded by rolling hills and beautiful sunsets, and the Montana sky was breathtaking. I walked to school in the late summer, through the fall, and now the winter. Soon it would be spring. Yes, my time in nature would surely change me for the better.

Back in my beadwork class, I decided on making a neck pouch. The last time I was in Billings, I had gone to the bead store and I bought yellow, green, and purple beads — the perfect color combination since Mardi Gras was right around the corner. In addition to the beads, I would decorate my neck pouch with elks' teeth. My neck pouch was going to require a lot more work than the medicine pouches I made during Native American Week. It would take me the whole semester to finish it, unlike just a day for making my medicine pouches. I wondered who I was going to give my neck pouch to. Since I was decorating my bag with elks' teeth, I decided that I would give it to my dentist, Dr. Van, back in Santa Clarita. He had been my dentist for twenty years, and yes, I even missed him too.

After a few classes, I began to realize that there was so much more to beadwork than just creating a pretty design. While I was learning the basics, something much deeper was beginning to evolve. I started to notice many similarities between beadwork and meditation. I had been going to meditation classes in Los Angeles for quite a few years and I really missed them. I realized that my beadwork class was much like meditation; both required concentration. It was almost impossible to do beadwork and think about something else. While beadwork involves working with the fingers, it is first done in the mind and that is what meditation is, working with the mind and not letting anything else come in. When I was doing my beadwork, I had to concentrate on sewing the beads onto the material and not let anything else interfere with that thought. To me that was meditation. In practical terms, when I concentrated fully on what was in front of me, I got more done and my bead rows were straight. If I lost my focus, my bead rows were crooked and I had to start over.

There were days when I went to beadwork class and for whatever reason, I just couldn't concentrate. This happened a lot when I tried to meditate too. But just like meditation, if I couldn't concentrate on my beadwork it was okay because it was the effort that counted. I had to learn to be patient with myself.

In addition to creating a piece of beadwork, we also had to write a reflection paper about the class. I wrote about the spirituality of beadwork. One of my students saw it on my desk and asked if he could read it. He was really impressed with it. I remember telling me, "Ms. Wagner, this is really good!"

Then there was the moment of truth. One day I showed my beadwork to my students and they started laughing, but not in a mean way. I understood why they were laughing. My beadwork did look a little funny. A lot of my rows were crooked. One of my students asked me if she could straighten out my rows for me. "You would do that for me?"

"Yes, Ms. Wagner I would do that for you."

"Why are you being so nice to me?"

"Because Ms. Wagner, you're having so much trouble with your beadwork."

I let her take my neck pouch home with her and she came back the next day with a couple of rows done. Her beadwork was beautiful. When I asked her if she could do a couple more for me, she said, "Of course."

She brought my neck pouch back the next day and the additional rows were just as beautiful as the first rows she had done.

"Thank you so much! You made my neck pouch look so pretty. Then she said to me, "Ms. Wagner, do you want me to finish it for you?"

"Oh! You would do that for me?"

"Yes, but just promise me one thing."

I couldn't imagine what she meant. "What is it?" I asked.

She hesitated and then said, "Just don't tell Philippe."

"Why not?" I was excited to tell Philippe how much she had helped me. I thought he might give her extra credit or something, but now I was concerned.

"Because Ms. Wagner, last year I did beadwork for another teacher and Philippe got mad at me and told me not to do that, but you were having so much trouble and your rows were so crooked I wanted to help you. So don't tell him, okay?"

Well, I knew that Philippe wouldn't get mad at her. It just wasn't his disposition or his teaching style. He wanted each student to do their own work. Whether crooked or straight, it would be their own original piece. It was the process, not just the product. But I had other motives. I intended on giving the pouch to my dentist, Dr. Van, back in Santa Clarita and I didn't want to give him something crooked. I wanted it to look really nice and authentic.

I told her I wouldn't say a word. She was very sweet and very helpful to me and I didn't want to break her trust. Plus, while she was helping me with my beadwork, I was trying to help her gain confidence and self-esteem. At the beginning of every period after our meditation, I always required a student to read in front of the class. She never wanted to read. I never gave her a hard time about it, but when her mother came in for her parent conference we talked about it. I didn't know if her daughter was embarrassed, shy, or just plain couldn't read, so I gave her mother the text to practice with her daughter at home. That strategy worked. One day she got up and read in front of the whole class. I was so proud of her and of myself. I was so glad that I let the student come to her own terms and read when she felt comfortable. I would like to think that I helped her develop self-esteem and she helped me with my beadwork.

One Saturday, I was working in my classroom and Philippe stopped by and we chatted a bit. He had been on the reservation for seven years and he told me how hard it had been for him in the beginning. I could relate. I asked him how he dealt with it and he told me the sweat lodges were a big help. I had gone to quite a few sweat lodges in the beginning of the year, but now with the snow, it was hard to find the rocks to heat. As a result, there hadn't been any sweats for a few months. Even though I hadn't gone to a sweat in quite some time, I thought back to the "womb" experience I was having here in Montana. What did I have to show for being here? Aside from taking classes and going to sweat lodge ceremonies and healing ceremonies and powwows, what was going to come out of all of this?

Philippe and I continued talking for a while longer and the one thing he said that resonated with me was the same thing Paul had told me months earlier — that no one chooses to come to the reservation, one is called to the reservation to do something special. I still hadn't figured out what that was.

CHAPTER TWENTY-EIGHT

A THOUSAND CRANES

The reservation started to thaw, and just as Black Elk had predicted, the long winter helped to heal the past. Ever since I had directed the play *A Thousand Cranes* at the all-girls school where I didn't "fit in," cranes seemed to pop up everywhere. They were a constant reminder of what I had and what I had lost. That had been my dream job and when they didn't renew my contract, I was devastated.

Those little paper cranes that for so many symbolized Sadako's story of determination, for me brought nothing but heartache until one day when I walked into the art room and something in the corner of the room caught my eye. Hanging from the ceiling was the most beautiful crane mobile ever. Cranes of all different sizes made with origami sheets, each one with their own unique colorful pattern and design were intertwined with beads of various shapes held together by a spiral wired base. I loved it and I wanted it.

I asked the art teacher, "Who made that beautiful crane mobile? I love it!"

She looked at me and with pride for her student said, "Oh, that was Lucy."

Oh great, I had just lost my bargaining power. A couple of days earlier, I took the kids over to the chapel to meditate. On the way over Lucy must have been really upset with me or the church or somebody associated with the church because all the way over she kept saying, "I hate the Church. I hate the Catholic Church." And she said it within earshot. She wanted me to hear her. I didn't respond. I basically ignored her and that made her say even louder, "I hate the Church. I hate the Catholic Church." So I doubted that she would ever want to give up her beautiful crane mobile to her religion teacher, but I asked anyway, "Do you think Lucy would want to sell it to me?"

She thought about it, "Hmm ... I know it has a lot of sentimental value to her. I don't think she would want to sell it, but it can't hurt to ask."

"I want to be fair, how much should I offer her?"

"Well, with the cost of materials and for the time she put into it, I'd say $50 would be a fair price."

A couple days later Lucy came into my classroom when no one else was there. She approached my desk with her head bowed, "Ms. Wagner, I'm really sorry I said those things the other day."

"What things?" I had forgotten her tirade from a few days earlier.

"When I said that I hated the Catholic Church. I'm sorry I said that. I really didn't mean it. I didn't mean to hurt you."

"You didn't hurt me. You really didn't."

"I know I hurt you and I'm really sorry I said that."

I insisted, "Lucy, you didn't hurt me and to be honest with you, I say the same thing too sometimes."

She was shocked, "You do?"

"Yeah, everybody says that at some point. You don't even have to be sorry for it. You were just being honest."

She breathed a sigh of relief.

"Lucy, I have something to ask you. The other day when I was in the art room I saw your crane mobile. The art teacher told me that it meant a lot to you, but if you ever want to sell it, I would be interested in buying it."

"You would?" she said excitedly.

"Yes, I love it. I think it's beautiful!"

"How much will you give me for it?"

I looked at her and asked, "Does $50.00 sound fair?"

"I'll take it." She didn't hesitate for a second.

"Lucy, are you sure?"

"Yes, I'm sure."

"As soon as I get a ride up to the bank, I will get the money for you."

That week Lucy came in my classroom every day, "Did you go to the bank, yet?" It took a few days, but I finally got a ride up to the bank.

She got her $50.00 and I got a beautiful crane mobile. She was happy that her art actually brought in money and I was happy that I could finally look at a crane and not feel sad about losing the job that I loved.

CHAPTER TWENTY-NINE

BLOOM WHERE YOU ARE PLANTED

I had been on the reservation for six months and I was still trying to figure out why I was there and what I was supposed to do. I thought back to my time at Daniel Murphy Catholic High School — the school that closed down in 2008. The principal wanted to make a time capsule, a video, about the school — its history, its alumni, its current students, and its closure. Since I was teaching the broadcast journalism class, the project fell to me. Luckily, a parent of one of my students was a television director and producer. We teamed up and working with the students we produced a documentary about the school. Even though the school was closing, I enjoyed every moment working on that project. I even remember one of my students saying to me, "Ms. Wagner, you're really happy working on your documentary, aren't you?"

We showed the documentary on graduation night and *NBC4 News* covered the event. The *Los Angeles Times* wrote a feature article about the school's closing and the film that the students produced. The film later won an award at the Oxnard Student Film Festival. That was a happy time for me and that's what I really wanted to be doing. And yet, I was so far away from it all. I wanted to be working with creative people in Los Angeles, working on documentaries and learning about film. But sometimes in life you think you are so far away from where you want to be and then you suddenly realize you are exactly where you're meant to be and something magical happens.

As I was walking home from school one night I thought of that saying, "Bloom where you are planted." I looked down at the snow and the frozen ground beneath it and said, "Thank you Lord, for giving me such fertile ground to bloom in." As soon as I said that, an image of a beautiful orange crocus coming up through the snow popped into my head. And then I got it — my reason for being on the reservation! I could do a documentary about the school —

student life, activities, the mission statement. That was it! After months of not knowing, struggling with inner turmoil, I finally knew why I was here on the reservation. Paul was right. My soul had called me here to do something special for these kids and I finally figured out what it was. I was to do a film about them and for them!

At first, I wasn't sure how people were going to react to it. This was a reservation in Montana, not a film school in Hollywood. I didn't dare mention it to the principal. I was finally on his good side. I didn't want to blow it with my idea of making a documentary during class time.

One afternoon I stopped in the development office and I casually mentioned my idea to one of the managers. He loved it! Even though I had his support, there were a couple of logistical hoops I had to jump through. While I had taught broadcast journalism and worked with directors and producers, the schools I had worked at previously had studios and software equipment. This school didn't even have a camera. 'What were the chances of getting a camera?' I wondered. I went to the librarian and asked him if there was any possibility of getting a video camera. To my utter amazement, he had just ordered two! All I had to do was to wait. It was unbelievable how things started to fall into place. It was as if a driving force was behind the entire project and I was just along for the ride.

A few days later the cameras arrived, not really the type of cameras that I was used to working with. One was a small camcorder and the other one was a flip camera, but I always say, "Work with what you've got." I brought the cameras into the classroom, but before we started filming, I had to smooth over a few things. Some of my students were a bit hesitant and I understood why. There was a history of exploitation regarding photography in Indian country. I remembered Ken telling me that in the late nineteenth and early twentieth centuries photographs of Native Americans were in high demand among white settlers. Photographers often took advantage of the situation and profited from the sale of Native American photos. A hundred years later, suspicions lingered. Aware of this, I assured my students that they would play a part in front of the camera and behind the camera; filming on location and then reviewing it in the classroom. This was their project and they would learn in the process. I told them that we might even enter it into a film festival. With that I gained their approval and full cooperation. And now for my next step, I had to teach the students the fundamentals of filming.

This was second semester and I was teaching the New Testament, so I incorporated video production into the class. I started by giving them a few small scenes from the Bible. I would assign parts, the students would rehearse their lines, and then we would go out on location and film their performances. I even went over to the thrift shop and got a box of clothes donated for their wardrobe changes.

For one class, we went over to the church and we filmed the Wedding of Cana. For another group, we went over to the pool and reenacted Jesus getting baptized in the Jordan. We had a cemetery located on the far side of the campus and I wanted to reenact Lazarus being raised from the dead, but I didn't want to do anything sacrilegious, so I went to see Father Paschal. Father Paschal had been a blessing to me ever since the day I met him in the parking lot when I came up for my interview. I looked forward to his sermons every Sunday. Sometimes it sounded almost as though they were written specifically for me. It was amazing how he did this. No matter what I was feeling or experiencing throughout the week Father Paschal's sermons always seemed to shed some light on my situation. He had helped me earlier in the year when I was teaching a course on the Sacraments.

Back at Santa Maria de las Rosas, the archdiocese had prescribed a guide for teaching the Sacraments. It worked in Los Angeles, but it was corny and I knew it would never fly on the reservation, so I went to see Father Paschal for advice. He gave me a copy of *The Pipe and Christ* by William Stolzman. The book was the culmination of a six-year dialogue between Lakota Medicine Men and Catholic leaders. It was a comparative study between Lakota traditions and rituals and Catholic Sacraments. It was a great resource for me. Now I needed his help again.

"Father, I have been doing some video work with the students and they really love it."

"What sort of things are you doing?" he inquired with a bit of curiosity.

"Well, I give them scenes from the New Testament and they have to reenact them. They memorize their lines and then we go out on location and shoot the scene."

"Oh! That sounds like a lot of fun."

"Father, I want to go over to the cemetery and film the scene of Lazarus being raised from the dead, but I don't want to do anything sacrilegious."

"Oh, that's fine, Luella, you can go over to the cemetery and film. That's fine."

"So I have your blessing, Father?" I wanted to make sure I had his blessing. Just in case someone complained or questioned what I was doing I could say Father Pascal said it was okay and he even gave me his blessing.

And then he gave me a reaffirming, "Yes, Luella you have my blessing." That's all I needed.

Next class period, I assigned parts for Lazarus, Mary, Martha, and Jesus. We wrapped one of the students in strips of cloth to make him look like Lazarus and then we went over to the cemetery. He got in position behind one of the tombstones. As Jesus, played by one of the students, was walking in the distance, two students who were playing Mary and Martha came crying, "Master, Master, your friend Lazarus is dying. Come quickly."

Jesus took another four days to get there and by the time he arrived, Lazarus was already dead and buried. Still in character, Jesus cried out, "Lazarus, come forth." At that moment the student playing Lazarus came out from behind the tombstone. It was actually quite funny. It was one of the best Bible reenactments I had done so far. The kids were learning their lines, learning how to work in front of the camera and behind it. Plus, I was enjoying my teaching. After we filmed, we would go back to the classroom and watch it on the SMART Board. Everybody was having a good time.

While all this was going on, I avoided the principal like the plague. It was a pretty big campus and I always kept my eyes out for him. He was easy to spot, even a mile away. He was tall and bald. If I got the slightest glimpse of him in the distance, I would immediately walk in the opposite direction, even if it meant that I had to walk around the entire campus. I hadn't run into him lately, or gotten an email or even a note in my teacher mailbox. It was great. Then one day while I was sitting in my classroom, during my prep period, the door opened and there he was. I immediately thought, 'Here goes my reason for being here.'

I don't know which is worse, when you get called to the principal's office or when they come over to you because then you are caught completely off guard. He walked straight over to my desk. I didn't even have time to think. "Ms. Wagner, I heard that you had a camera… and that you were taking the kids out of the classroom. You took a group of students over to the pool… you took another group of students over to the chapel. I heard that you had even taken some of your students over to the cemetery and that you were filming. Is that true?"

For a split second, I thought about saying, "Me… doing filming? Who told you that?" I just looked down. I knew I was caught. I knew it was over. I said, "Yes, that's true. Are you okay with that?"

He paused and said, "Ms. Wagner… I think… I think that is…Ms. Wagner, I think that is awesome."

"You do?"

"Oh, yes, anything "hands-on" that you can get the kids involved with is awesome."

That's one scene I wish I had gotten on film. At first I didn't know how to respond. Then he asked me, "So tell me what you are doing with the students."

I was taken a bit by surprise, but I was able to come up with a quick response, "Well, I assign short scenes from the Bible for them to rehearse and then we go out on location and film the scenes. We come back into the classroom and then we watch what we did on the SMART board."

"And the kids are learning?"

"Oh, yes! They are learning the Bible stories, but they are also learning how to use the camera. They are learning different camera angles, when to zoom in and out, how to get the most out of the scene."

"That's exactly what we need to be doing with our students."

And then I sprung it on him. "I was thinking about doing something on a different level with the students. When I worked at Daniel Murphy Catholic High School, I produced a documentary about the school. The school was closing down and the principal wanted to preserve its memory with a time capsule, a video. I worked with a director and along with my broadcast journalism class we were able to produce a documentary about the history and the traditions of the school. The film even won an award at the Oxnard Student Film Festival. I would like to do something like that here. The students would be involved in all aspects, in front of the camera and behind it. They would be involved in interviewing teachers, students, and alumni."

He loved the idea. "As long as you stay on curriculum, I'm fine with it."

So, he gave me the green light. This was my reason for being here.

CHAPTER THIRTY

FLIGHT OF THE BUTTERFLIES

Spring finally came to the reservation. The temperatures warmed up, the snow began to melt, the days grew longer. The signs and sounds of springtime started to sneak up everywhere. The cottonwood tree that I passed by every day on my way to school slowly started to show small sprouts of new life. I loved that cottonwood tree. It was such a testimony to the power of nature and the subtlety of growth. Each day new leaves appeared methodically and beautifully, demonstrating to the world the joy of creation. For months it stood bare, a constant reminder of the grim austerity of the winter season. And then by nature's magic, the tree was in full bloom, just like me.

Being on the reservation, I had grown accustomed to the deafening silence. For the longest time the only thing that broke the silence was the crunch of snow beneath my feet as I walked to and from school every day. And then one day as I was walking home from school it happened. It was as if the sky opened up with a sudden and spontaneous crack. I heard what I thought was a duck. Or maybe it was a goose. I didn't know what it was; all I knew was that it was some kind of a bird announcing the end of winter and the beginning of spring. It was a loud "Honk." It was as if that bird was talking directly to me, letting me know that spring had sprung. It reminded me of the Celtic symbol of the Holy Spirit. While Catholics typically view the dove as the symbol of the Holy Spirit, in the Celtic tradition the Holy Spirit is represented by a wild goose. That was it! It was a wild goose that I heard! Hallelujah!

The next day, I told the kids what I had heard the day before and they agreed that it probably was a wild goose. Over the next few days I became very conscious of birds as I walked to and from school. One morning I noticed a tiny enclave of birds on the ledge of the school auditorium. Every day after that I would stop and talk to them. "I am so glad to see you! Where have you been all these months? It's been really quiet around here without you. Got any plans for the summer?" And they would chirp back as if they had understood every word I said. I didn't care if anyone saw me talking to the birds. They were beautiful to me and I wanted to let them know how much I loved them. I looked forward to my chat with them every morning. I understood the whole St. Francis thing. You know, talking to the animals. Sometimes they were a lot easier to converse with than human beings.

That wasn't the only bird sanctuary on campus. I found another chorus of birds that had taken up residence in a shrub located right outside the development office. During the winter it was a bare bundle of branches, now it was an amphitheater with a live concert every morning filled with little tiny birds singing their hearts out. One morning I just stopped and stared at the magnificence of it all. Each bird was perched on its own special branch as if nature assigned the perfect spot for each individual pitch. Before I came to the reservation, I used to hear birds all the time and it was just background noise, now it uplifted my soul. It took a brutal Montana winter for me to truly appreciate all the gifts that nature had to offer.

There was an open field behind my classroom that I never paid much attention to. For months it lay dormant covered in snow, but once the snow melted, the most dazzling display of nature's delights danced right in front of me. One afternoon I stepped outside my classroom and I looked out into the field and I saw two butterflies darting around each other. I thought I was so fortunate to have captured the sight of two butterflies, not one, but two! They were absolutely beautiful. I couldn't stop looking at them. How can one look at a butterfly and not feel joy? I thought to myself, 'My cocoon experience is coming to an end and now my butterfly adventure is about to begin.'

After school, I looked out at the field again and I couldn't believe the sight before me. It was almost as if it was a dream. The entire field was swarming with butterflies. I stood in total amazement at what was taking place before me — the movement of hundreds, possibly thousands of butterflies taking flight. I stared at the sight because I knew I would never see anything like it again. Just watching them elevated my entire being. I remembered Paul telling me once that after I made it through the long winter, I would have the best springtime of my life. He was right. This was like no other springtime I had ever experienced.

My cute little yellow house that had been surrounded by snow for months was now in the midst of a bed of matching yellow dandelions. I had never appreciated the beauty of dandelions before, but now they were radiant balls of sunshine saying "Good morning" to me every day as I left for school and "Welcome home" every night when I returned. I had never noticed, but when it gets dark, dandelions close up almost as if they are sleeping. It was just another one of nature's wonders that was so fascinating to me.

My students also alerted me to the reservation's unique way of announcing the coming of springtime. One day as I walked behind a couple of students I overheard one of them say to another one, "I'm so glad to see the mud."

I thought that was a weird comment. I was glad that the snow had melted and I could finally see the ground, but I wasn't necessarily happy about the mud. Every day I had to be really careful not to slip and fall in it. At least when I fell down in the snow, it was only water, but mud was a different story. Later that day I said to him, "Hey, I overheard you say that you were happy to see the mud."

"Yeah."

"Why?"

He looked at me and said, "Oh, Ms. Wagner, because it means the winter is over."

And then I said with such relief, "You're right! You are so right! The winter's over."

I had been through the coldest, darkest, longest winter of my life and it was over. It was finally over. Spring was here and so was the mud. I will never look at mud the same way again.

I started to feel like me again. I didn't know if it was because it was springtime, or because the weather was warming up, or because the birds were singing, or because it was staying light out late, or a combination of all those things. All I knew was that I felt a whole lot better than I did in January. I was so happy! I loved my life. I loved God. I loved everything that had happened to me. Everything.

I not only had a greater appreciation for nature, but I had an overwhelming sense of gratitude for my entire Montana experience. I never knew what I was capable of enduring until I came to the reservation. The reservation tested me in every way — physically, emotionally, mentally, and spiritually. I was a stronger person for it. Whether anyone recognized it or not didn't matter.

Now I had a very difficult decision ahead of me. The principal had offered me a contract for next year and I had to decide if I was going to stay another year or not. The thought of going back to California without any prospect of a job was scary. The country was still in a recession and my job prospects were just as bleak as the year before. But could I make it in Montana for another year? The winters were brutal. I was torn. Here in Montana, I had a bonafide job offer. In California, I didn't know what I would find. I tried to look at it from every angle and I just got more and more confused. I needed to talk to somebody. I called Paul and as usual, he suggested the metaphysical approach.

"Luella, if you don't have to make a decision right away, try to relax with it and allow your heart to guide you. What I mean by that is, what are you feeling? What is your intuition telling you? Are you excited about future possibilities in Montana? Or is returning to California more appealing? Try to seek some spiritual guidance and be open to a response in some form. Sit quietly and ask the universe, 'What do you want me to do?' Ask the universe, 'Where is it that you want me to go?'" He told me to wait patiently and the universe would make it clear what I was to do, but I didn't feel like waiting patiently for an answer. I wanted somebody to tell me what to do, right now.

After my conversation with Paul, I called my good friend Bev. She, like Paul, also was very spiritual in her approach to life. She told me to seek guidance from my angels. I didn't have patience for that either. I decided to call Dolores. She would give me practical advice.

"Dolores, I'm thinking about staying another year."

"What? You're thinking about staying another year?"

"You send me emails all the time about how cold it is and how you think you're going to die and now you want to stay there another year?"

"Dolores, to be honest, it's pretty good right now. The principal likes me. The kids like me. I am doing a documentary. And the snow is almost all melted. Maybe I'm supposed to stay here another year. Maybe I'm supposed to stay here for the rest of my life."

"Luella, come home. You went there for a year to teach those kids and you probably did things with those kids that no other teacher would have done. You can come home now."

I hesitated, "That's just it, Dolores. I don't know how I am going to get home."

After a brief pause, Dolores said, "I'll come up and get you."

"You will? You'll do that for me? You'll really do that for me?"

"Yeah, I'll do it for you."

The next day Dolores called me. "Okay, I got online and I reserved the U-Haul. I'll fly up on Saturday, June 4th, get the U-Haul, drive over to the reservation, and on Sunday we'll high-tail it out of there. You're coming home."

The decision was made. I was coming home, but not until I finished my documentary.

CHAPTER THIRTY-ONE

WE SHALL SURVIVE

I would be using class time to direct and produce the film, but since it was going to be about the school's mission statement, I wasn't taking away from the curriculum. I was actually enhancing it. By now my students were familiar with the camera, having worked in front of it and behind it. I wanted all of my students to participate in the production of the film, so I assigned each one of them different parts based on their skill sets.

I wanted teachers and staff to be a part of the documentary as well, so some students were involved in scheduling times when the teachers and members of the staff were available for filming, while other students wrote the questions for the students who would be conducting the interviews. In addition to interviewing teachers and staff, students would also be involved in interviewing each other and sharing their thoughts about the school.

The students did a fabulous job with the interviews. Father Paschal spoke about the challenges and hardships of living on the reservation, but he also spoke about the great faith and perseverance of the Natives. Sister Bernadette gave a detailed account of the history of the school and its patron saint, St. Labre. She explained that St. Labre became known as the pilgrim saint whose vocation was traveling from shrine to shrine on foot visiting the holiest places of Catholic spirituality.

Ken Kania, who had been at the school for thirty-six years, reminisced about his students. Philippe spoke about the importance of beadwork in the Native American tradition today. Ed, the math teacher, shared his faith journey and stressed the influence that faith plays in a student's education. Russ Alexander Ed.D. discussed the opportunities that were in place for Native American students when they left the reservation. Benji Headswift, the drum instructor, gave a powerful interview that explained the healing power of the drum beat. My students also interviewed the Crow and Cheyenne language instructors.

Many students were in front of the camera as well. Ty, one of the top basketball players, spoke not only about the sports program at the school, but the core value of integrity in playing the game. Chase talked about how the students supported one another in their studies, sports events, or with personal issues and problems. Andrea, a tenth grader, talked about the importance of stewardship. She worked in the afterschool program in the elementary school and helped the little ones with their homework in addition to coaching their basketball games.

I finally got to work with Rosalia Bad Horse. I had been so impressed with her grace and stature I just had to include her in my film. At first she was a little apprehensive and wanted to know what I was going to do with the film. When I told her that we were going to show it at the end of the year and maybe enter it into a film festival, she was onboard with the project. And she looked beautiful as Miss Northern Cheyenne Princess. Alexis Braided Hair, Miss St. Labre and Ivy Old Elk, Miss Kyi-Yo were also featured in the documentary.

I also wanted alumni to be part of the film. I was so fortunate that a former student, Lou Pavek, who had graduated from the school in the 1950s, still lived in town. When my students approached him with the idea of being in a documentary about the school, he was thrilled to be part of it.

As a tribute to the graduating class, each one of them had the chance to say their name, their tribe, and their future plans. And there was my challenge. I had one student who barely talked, now he had to speak for the video. He was the one who helped me up earlier in the year when I was slipping and sliding all over the place in my California boots. Trevor never spoke in class, but now I needed him to speak. It took several takes, but I never gave up on him. I knew he would come through and after several attempts he was able to say his name, his tribe, and his future aspirations.

When I first announced to my classes that I was doing a film, one of my students, Liz, a tenth grader approached me a few days later. "Ms. Wagner I really want to work with you on your documentary." Liz was quite shy, hardly ever spoke a word in class. I sometimes got the impression that she didn't like me. I couldn't imagine that she would want to be in front of the camera or even directing behind the camera and then she said, "I really want to edit it." I was flattered, but my original intention was to film as much as I could at the school and then bring back the footage to Los Angeles and have one of my editor friends do the final cut. There was no way was I going to put my documentary in the hands of a 14-year-old. I had to let her down easy because I didn't want to discourage her from future projects. I just looked at her and said, "Liz, I was going to have a professional editor back in Los Angeles do it."

She accepted it, but I felt terrible and then I said, "Liz, why don't you work on some of the Bible scenes that we did in class. I'll give you those scenes to edit and let's see what you can do with them."

I didn't have any editing software, but Liz said she had a program on her computer that she could use. The next day, Liz came into my classroom, "Ms. Wagner, I edited those scenes for you."

"What? I only gave them to you yesterday."

"Yes, I know, but I worked on them all last night and I want to show them to you."

She showed me on the computer what she had done. I looked at her in amazement, "Liz, you can edit!"

I couldn't believe it! This 14-year-old student who sat in my class and hardly said a word all year, possessed the skill to edit.

"Yes, Ms. Wagner, that's what I was trying to tell you."

"Liz, do you feel confident editing the entire documentary?"

I didn't understand editing, nor did I want to understand it.

"Yes, Ms. Wagner I can edit the entire documentary."

"Okay Liz, I am going to have to get some really good editing software for you to use. Let me look into it."

I knew I would have to buy it myself. If I asked the administration, it would have to be put in next year's budget and get board approval before I would see any money at all. Plus, I had to finish the film by the end of the school year. Dolores was coming to pick me up in June. Remember Adele, who I met on the flight up for my interview? Fortunately, I still had her contact information and I knew she could give me some advice. She gave me two options: Final Cut Pro or Sony Vegas Pro Tem. When I mentioned it to Liz and asked her what she wanted, she said, "Ms. Wagner both of these are really expensive and I don't want you to spend all your money on it."

Earlier in the year, the counseling office had asked us for the names of all the colleges we graduated from. They made banners for all the teachers' alma maters and I hung mine on the wall right next to my desk. When Liz said she didn't want me to spend all my money on editing software, I pointed to the banners — Boston University, UCLA, and New York University. "Liz, do you see all those university logos over there?"

She nodded. And then I said, "Every single one of those college degrees is paid for. I think I can afford editing software."

We decided on Sony Vegas Pro Tem. I pulled out my credit card and called in the order. It was a big investment, but I was confident that Liz could learn the program and use it for the documentary. About a week later, the editing software arrived in the mail. I was clueless as to how to install it, but luckily, the computer guy in the technology department was able to get it up and running. Liz and I both sat there and waited as he installed the program on my computer and then he asked Liz, "Have you ever used this before?"

She answered, "No."

I got a queasy feeling. I had just charged $700.00 to my credit card and now I wasn't sure if Liz could pull it off. As soon as the computer guy left my classroom, Liz sat down at my computer and within a few minutes I had complete confidence in her editing abilities. Sometimes I look back in amazement. What were the chances that I would go to Montana, produce a student documentary and just happen to have an incredibly talented student who could edit like a pro?

While Liz and I worked on editing the film after school, a little angel would pop in to see if we needed anything. Her name was Holly. She was the music teacher and it was her first teaching assignment. She was a wonderful teacher as I could tell from the phenomenal job she did with the Christmas musical. She had an instinct for music and she was demanding of her students. Plus, she was a true friend and a real blessing. She would always stop by my classroom and ask if there was anything she could help out with. Since I didn't have a car and she did, she would drive me up to Michelle's Munchies and I would get dinner for Liz, Holly, myself and whoever else was working with us. I appreciated Holly so much, not just for giving me a ride up to Michelle's Munchies, but for her support, kindness, and friendship.

I really believed that this was the reason why I was called to the reservation. Earlier in the year Paul kept telling me that I was there to do something special for "those kids" and I had to figure out what it was and that I couldn't come home until I did. So I knew I had to finish this film before Dolores picked me up, but I was running out of time. We were planning to show the film for the entire student body the last day of school, but we only had two weeks of school left to finish the editing and sound mixing. And then I got hit with a deluge, literally.

Because we had so much snow that winter, once the temperatures warmed up the snow melted and caused huge amounts of flooding on the reservation and in nearby towns. I was so happy that it had finally warmed up, but I had no idea how much water there would be when the snow melted. There was even talk that the village might be evacuated. Before leaving school for the weekend, I had to move all the computer equipment in my classroom as far off the floor as possible. I went home that night hoping and praying that my cats and I would not have to evacuate. Over the weekend, the waters began to recede, but the flooding caused roads and highways to be shut down. On Monday, the students from Crow Agency didn't make it to school. None of the buses could pick them up because of the flooding. Liz was stuck in Crow Agency and I was worried that she wouldn't make it back to finish the editing in time for the last day of school. 'Oh no,' I thought, 'this was my reason for being here, and now it's not going to happen.'

I didn't have a clue about editing and I couldn't entrust it to any other student. I panicked. Every morning, I raced down the halls anxiously looking and asking for Liz. "Have you seen Liz? Has anyone seen Liz this morning?"

"No, Ms. Wagner, I don't think she's coming in today."

Another student would say, "No, she's not here today."

For a whole week every morning, I darted through the halls looking for Liz to see if she had made it to school. She never did.

I had this sickening feeling that I wasn't going to finish my documentary and I wouldn't accomplish my purpose for being called to the reservation. All my work, all my students' work, all the time and effort that was put into my documentary, not to mention the software I had charged on my credit card, was all for nothing. I thought of all these outlandish ways to get Liz back to school. I even had the thought of renting a helicopter and airlifting her back.

That weekend the flooding seemed to subside and the roads and highways were reopened, so there was a good chance that Liz would be back in school on Monday. But would we have enough time to finish editing the documentary? It was really cutting it close, no pun intended. Monday morning, I raced through the halls again looking for Liz and then I spotted her long blond hair in the distance. Her blond locks in the sea of dark-haired students was as obvious as the principal's bald head. I was never so happy to see a student as I was to see Liz. I ran up to her, "Liz, can we finish editing the documentary by the end of the year?"

"Yes, Ms. Wagner we can finish it."

"You're sure, Liz?"

"Yes, I'm sure, Ms. Wagner."

I had full confidence in Liz's ability to edit, but I was worried that we didn't have enough time to complete the video in just a few days. But Liz handled it like a pro and we were able to show it the last day of school. I was so impressed with her composure and her ability to work under pressure. Plus, she had to deal with me every five minutes, "We're going to finish this, right? We're going to finish, right? You'll be able to get it done by the end of the week, right?"

She would always respond with such calmness and certainty, "Yes, Ms. Wagner."

I later asked her if she would want to work with me again. She paused, thought about it, and then she said very calmly, "Maybe."

Andrea, my student who worked in the afterschool program, took on the role of publicity. She volunteered to make fliers for the film and she posted them up at the Trading Post in town. We invited everyone in the area to come. It was the first movie premiere ever held in Ashland, Montana.

We called the film *We Shall Survive* because the school had been around since 1884. The students dedicated it to Father Emmett, the priest who came to the reservation in the 1950s and transformed the school into what it is today. Father Emmett was invited to the premiere as the guest of honor.

CHAPTER THIRTY-TWO

THANK YOU

The last day of school all the high school students filed into the auditorium and watched *We Shall Survive*. While the students watched the film, I watched them. After months of sacrifice, effort, and hard work it all paid off. It was the first time in my academic career that I had captured the attention of that many students for that length of time. It was an incredibly rewarding moment for me as a teacher.

When the film was over, the students formed a line to personally thank me and to say good-bye. One of the elders, who I had invited into my class earlier in the year to talk to my students about the Wheel of Life, came up to me and gave me a big hug. She thanked me for all I had done for the students and then she said something I will never forget.

"I know you are leaving and I understand why you want to go back home, but you can always come back. We will always have a place for you." After being told at previous schools that I didn't fit and that I didn't know how to teach, I finally felt vindicated.

Ed, the math teacher, came up to say good-bye. I looked at him and said, "You know Ed, this was the reason why I came to the reservation." He looked at me and said, "No it wasn't."

"What do you mean, that it's not the reason why I was called here? What are you talking about?" I was in a state of shock. Was I supposed to do something else on the reservation? Did I get it all wrong?

Ed looked at me and in his true missionary spirit said, "God called you to the reservation to bring you closer to Him."

"Well, He has a funny way of doing it. For a while I wasn't even talking to Him."

After the premiere of *We Shall Survive* I headed back to my classroom and began the task of tearing everything down for one last time. Wyatt needed some extra credit, so he came by and helped me take down all the posters, pictures, and drawings I had on the walls and on the ceiling. It was a lot easier breaking down my classroom this year. I thought back to the year before and how difficult it had been to take it all down. But rather than fill up with sentimental attachment, I knew that every time I had to tear something down, something new would pop up in its place. This time, I was leaving on my own terms.

Just as I finished packing up my things, the door opened. Guess who! It was the principal. I immediately thought, 'Now what! What could he possibly have to say to me now? I've just gone through the most difficult year of my life. I am proud of the work I did with my students and I have a documentary to show for it. What could he possibly want from me now?'

He sat down at one of the student's desks and I thought, 'Oh, no! He's going to be here for a while.' And then he said, "Ms. Wagner, I want to thank you for all you did for our kids, here on the reservation."

At first I didn't know what to say and then the words blurted out … "Well, I really should be the one thanking you. You allowed me to do something really special with my students and most principals wouldn't have given me the freedom to do that. I really should be the one thanking you."

There was a silence and then he asked, "Do you know what you are going to do yet?"

"No, I don't. I don't even know if I am still going to teach … but I was wondering wherever I go, if I could use you as a reference."

"Absolutely." There was a pause and then, "When do you leave?"

"My friend Dolores comes up tomorrow, we pack up the U-Haul and then we leave the next day."

"You're not staying for June?"

"Why? What happens in June?"

"That's tick season!"

My time in Montana was like the plagues of Egypt. Cold, snow, ice, floods, mud ... now ticks?

As I made that one final walk home, I gazed across the expansive campus that had been my refuge for the past nine months. What was once a thick blanket of snow, was now a sprawling sea of green grass. The small footpath surrounded by snow that I walked every day to my classroom was now an expansive sidewalk dotted with giant planters filled with radiant red geraniums. I thought of my mother. She loved geraniums and she used to put pots like that on our front porch every spring. I was certain that this was a sign from her. She had died twenty-six years ago and even though I knew she was always with me, the subtle signs of her presence that popped up every so often always brought me joy.

And then it hit me, the whole womb experience. My nine months in Montana was over and now I had a sign from my mother letting me know that a new life for me was about to begin. I did not know what was in store for me, but now I could face the future with an open heart, seek new experiences with an open mind, and embrace my destiny with open arms! What a difference a year makes! I looked to my future with hope and optimism that something grand would come from my Montana experience.

My endurance of the long blistering winter months did not go unnoticed. That last week of school as I was walking home, one of my neighbors was standing in his driveway and he yelled over, "Hey, congratulations!"

I yelled back, "For what?"

"You did it!"

"Did what?"

"You survived a Montana winter."

I chuckled. "Yeah, I survived a Montana winter, the coldest one in fifty years!"

I know one thing — I couldn't have survived it without my cats. There's just something about coming home to that unconditional love every night that keeps you going. If anything had happened to them while I was on the reservation, it would have been over for me. I wouldn't have even come home. I would have just walked over to the cemetery and laid down and died. Actually, I would have turned it into a lesson plan. "Hey, kids we're going over to the cemetery to dig a hole. Guess who's getting in it. It's okay, you can throw dirt on me."

The next morning, I couldn't wait for the U-Haul to pull up into the driveway. I knew Dolores would be coming late in the afternoon so I sat on my couch, staring out the window as I had done so many days before, envisioning her pulling up into my driveway. Now it was actually going to happen. I sat there and waited and waited and then the U-Haul showed up. That image will be ingrained in my mind forever. I ran out to meet her and as she stepped out of the U-Haul her first words were, "The weather up here is beautiful!"

We packed up the U-Haul that night. Sunday morning as we pulled out of the driveway I gave one last look to my little yellow house that had been my sanctuary, my hiding place for two hundred and eighty-four days. In my heart I whispered, "Thank you. Thank you for sheltering me. Thank you for keeping me warm and for keeping my cats warm. Thank you for giving me silence at the end of the day so I could read and write, and thank you for giving me a good night's sleep and for keeping me safe. But most importantly, thank you for giving me a place where I could search the inner depths of my soul and discover the strength and resilience that I never knew I had."

As we rounded the corner, I took one last glance at the big cottonwood tree that I had passed by every day during those cold winter months looking for a sign of hope, a sign of spring, a sign of life. The tree that once stood bare was now filled with big beautiful leaves that graced my front yard while its branches seemed to wave, "So long, so long."

I had to make one last stop. I had to drop my keys off at John Walks Along's house. Michael, my student, met me at the door. "Are you coming to the powwow?"

"I don't know about this year, maybe next year!"

I thought it was quite appropriate that the first Indian I met on the reservation was John Walks Along and now the last one I saw was his son, Michael.

I jumped back in the U-Haul and as Dolores likes to say, "We hightailed out of there." There were flood warnings still in effect and we weren't taking any chances of getting stuck in a flood.

The ride back took on an entirely different sentiment. I was no longer filled with anxiety or uncertainty. Even though I had no job, no income, I had no fear. It would work itself out.

Driving back I had to ask, "Hey Dolores, why did you do it? I mean, why did you drive me up here?"

"Well, I knew you needed help. That night when you came back from your interview, I knew that for whatever reason you had to come here and who else would drive you and your three cats up to Montana in a U-Haul?"

"Yeah, you're right Dolores, I couldn't have done it without you."

"So, did you do what you were supposed to do?" Dolores asked.

"Well, it took me a while to figure it out, but I did a documentary with the students and we showed it the last day of school. I think the students will remember it for a long time. I am proud of the work I did, but I somehow think that it's not over yet, that there is still something else for me to do. I just don't know what it is yet. Time will tell."

And then I got philosophical. "You know, when I came up here, I was mad and angry about what had happened to me. I was mad that the only job I could find in the entire country was on an Indian reservation in the middle of nowhere, but you know what, it turned out to be the best job in the world for me."

It took us four days to get home. We followed the same procedure as before with my cats. Each pet-friendly hotel, I would take the cats in one at a time as Dolores waited in the U-Haul and I would repeat the procedure in reverse when we checked out the next morning.

We took a different route going home. This time we traveled through the western part of Montana, then Idaho, Oregon, Nevada, and then home. On our first stop in California, I got out of the U-Haul and kissed the ground.

CHAPTER THIRTY-THREE

SOME GOOD NEWS AND SOME SAD NEWS

Back in Woodland Hills, we unpacked the U-Haul and brought it back the next day. The same guy who I rented the U-Haul from back in August was still there. He remembered me. How could he forget! I wasn't quite as frantic returning the U-Haul as I was renting it.

One of the very first things I did once I got home was to get my hair done. That was the longest time in twenty years that I had ever gone without coloring my hair. I hadn't seen Gail, my hair stylist, for almost a year and as fate would have it, she was on vacation. Luckily, she had a backup hair stylist so I went to him. He told me my hair hadn't been colored in so long, it was like "virgin hair."

The first few weeks back were an adjustment to say the least. I remember that first time I went to Ralph's supermarket. I just stood and stared at all the fresh fruit and vegetables so neatly arranged in perfectly stacked rows. Vegetables never looked so good. And there were so many of them! I didn't want to eat them, I just wanted to stare at them. As I walked up and down the long aisles filled with every imaginable item, I reminisced about the Amish store with all the dented canned goods and expired salad dressings.

I got a pizza at Ameci's and a veggie taco at Baja Buds. I went to Gelson's and feasted on the salad bar like never before. It was so good to be back home. Many of the same people were there, just a little older. They must have looked at me and thought I had aged ten years, but with a little bit of sunshine and some healthy eating I was back to myself in no time. That summer, I went to the beach a lot. I think I had missed the ocean more than anything else.

I was even happy to see my dentist! I brought him the medicine cedar bag with the elks' teeth on it that I made for him during my beadwork class. He liked it and hung it in a special place in his office.

A few weeks after being back, I went out to my car and I noticed a grasshopper on the roof. "Well, look at you! You came all the way down here from Montana." Of course it wasn't the same one, but grasshopper was teaching me a lesson. I hop around a lot in life and that's okay. That's what I am supposed to do.

A few days later I was swimming in the pool and I noticed another grasshopper, but this one was dead in the water. I immediately thought, 'Oh no, is this another sign? Am I suddenly going to drown in the pool? Am I going to have a heart attack in the pool when no one is around and just sink to the bottom?' I cupped my hands and pulled the little guy out of the water. He was dead alright. And then I realized what the lesson was. Yes, I do hop around a lot, but someday it would all come to an end and I would rest in peace, but until that time I would just keep hopping. That was what I was created to do.

I had only been back for a few months when my little Juanita wasn't doing too good. She just wasn't herself. I took her to the vet and he ran several tests and there didn't appear to be anything serious or life-threatening. She had a little infection and he gave me some pills to give her, but getting a cat to swallow a pill is one of life's most difficult challenges. Even when I was sure I got her to swallow it, she would spit it back up. She was still eating, so I was able to hide it in her food, but I didn't see any improvement in her health. I sensed that she was getting toward the end, but I didn't want to accept it. I held out hope that she would soon be back to normal, but that was not to be. And then that day came. One morning, I just held her in my arms and she took her last breath. She had her little paw right over my heart. I was devastated.

Anyone who has lost a pet, knows the grief and sorrow that follows. At times it was unbearable. Even Tiger and Moo Moo shared in my grief.

A few weeks later I was over Dolores' house lamenting my loss. I told Dolores, "My little Juanita … my little Juanita … she got me up to Montana and back."

Dolores looked at me and said, "Juanita? Juanita gets all the credit for that? I drove you fifteen hundred miles in a U-Haul up to Montana and back, and Juanita gets all the credit for doing that?"

My friend Debbie once told me, "When God gives you a cross that is too heavy to carry, He will aways send you a Simon." That's why I called Dolores my Simone, because there was no way I could drive a U-Haul fifteen hundred miles to Montana with my three cats and back.

I often think back to when I came to California in the 1980s and started working at the Burbank Airport Hilton. I thought I was just looking for a job, but what I found was so much more — a friendship that would last a lifetime. I have often said, "Jobs come and go, but friendships last forever." You may have hundreds, or even thousands of friends on Facebook and Instagram, but I have discovered that if you find one good friend in life who will be willing to drive you fifteen hundred miles in a U-Haul you're pretty damn lucky. And for me that friend is Dolores.

Sadly, my Tiger passed away the following year. He was seventeen. He too passed away peacefully. How he loved Montana! I will always remember him looking out the window in the morning watching me go to school. When I rescued the both of them from the garage in Reseda, I never imagined that we would do a cross-country trip to Montana in a U-Haul. Two years after Tiger passed away, my little Moo Moo passed on. She was fourteen. To be honest, I don't think I would have made it through the reservation without them. They got me through the toughest, coldest, longest winter of my life. Without them to come home to every night, I don't think I would have lasted. They slept by my side, woke up with me every morning and kept me company through the whole two hundred and eighty-four days.

But life goes on. I hadn't been back long when I went to visit my friend Ray at Islands, the same restaurant where we had met over a year ago when I first told him about my idea of going to Montana. Our conversation was a lot different this time. I wasn't filled with worry or uncertainty about my fate, now I could look back with satisfaction knowing that I had made the right decision by going to the reservation. Driving back up the 405 freeway I saw the Montana Ave sign — the same sign that sent fear and anxiety through me, now made me laugh. And now the sign is gone.

Years later when I was driving up the 405 I couldn't find it. I got on and off the freeway several times looking for that sign, but it was gone. Was it all in my imagination? No, the California Department of Transportation did some upgrades and now the exit doesn't even exist and the sign was taken down. If they had done it years prior I might not have ever gone to Montana!

That Thanksgiving, George and Edie, the beautiful loving couple who encouraged me to go to the reservation when I was having all my doubts and apprehension, invited me and several other guests to their house for dinner. Everyone was so interested in my time in Montana. I began to understand that my Montana story wasn't over, that it would continue on indefinitely.

I visited Paul and as usual we had a long philosophical talk about life. It's amazing how people come in and out of your life at just the right moment, to console, advise, inspire, and motivate. I will always be so grateful for the conversations I had with Paul and his revelation to me that my soul had called me to the reservation to do something special for those kids. If it wasn't for those words I don't think I ever would have found my reason for being there.

In 2012, *We Shall Survive* was featured in the Loyola Marymount University Film Showcase, the same showcase as *The Way* with Martin Sheen and Emilio Estevez and *For Greater Glory* with Andy Garcia and Eva Longoria — something that I never could have imagined when I started out with a flip camera and no software equipment. I entered *We Shall Survive* into the Oxnard Student Digital Film Festival and it won in the News and Documentary

Division and they gave me a plaque and a T-shirt. While I appreciated the recognition, I remember thinking, 'I went through all that for a plaque and a T-shirt?'

I thought to call my good friend Roger. He always had words of wisdom for me. Roger had been my department chair when I taught at Notre Dame High School and even though I left Notre Dame, we remained friends over the years. A lot of time had passed since we last talked because he didn't even know I went to Montana. After sharing with him all my trials and tribulations, I said, "I still don't know why I had to go through everything I went through."

And Roger said, "Well, maybe it was to help other people who are going through something similar."

I brushed it off and thought, 'Yeah, right, someone loses their job, I can help them pack up the U-Haul and give them directions to the reservation.' As time went by I started to take what Roger said seriously and I decided to tell my story to as many people as possible. I began by giving local retreats and workshops in the Los Angeles area. I spoke to teachers, students, and catechists. Even Native Americans wanted to hear my story.

It was at the National Catholic Education Association Conference that I literally ran into the Monsignor, the one who would have nothing to do with me. While he wasn't able to attend my workshop, he did agree to meet with me a few weeks later. St. Theresa of Avila was right — "Patience obtains all things." It only took six years to get his attention. We had a long and contentious meeting, but in the end all was forgiven.

As I told my story at various venues, I was amazed at how many people came up to me after and thanked me and told me that they had gone through something similar. They didn't necessarily end up on an Indian reservation, but their lives did go through twists and turns and they didn't understand why. My story gave them hope and some parts even made them laugh. Roger was right! I was able to help people in a similar situation.

My story became a one-woman show entitled *Bloom Where You Are Planted* that I wrote and performed in. When I was walking through the snows of Montana I never dreamed I would perform in a show about the reservation at the Whitefire Theatre in Sherman Oaks. And it was a comedy! It is amazing how the things that caused me so much pain and sorrow could now make people laugh, and that made the experience all the more worthwhile.

I later wrote *The Seven Directions of the Medicine Wheel* about the lessons I learned from this Native American tradition. Adele, the woman who sat next to me on the plane when I went up for my interview, became my editor. I am still amazed at how a total stranger who I randomly sat next to on a plane became my loyal friend and confidante. What were the chances?

Many times I've called the reservation to see how things are going and there isn't a time when someone doesn't ask, "When are you coming back?"

I don't know if I will ever go back to the reservation, but in my mind, I go there every day. It was a life-changing experience and even years later I am still trying to come to terms with the full extent of it all. In spite of all the ups and downs that I felt living on the reservation, it was well worth it in so many ways.

A few weeks before I left Montana, I had a conversation with Sister Bernadette, the Mission Director, who had first interviewed me and eventually hired me. I told her that I was leaving the reservation, but I truly felt that I had been blessed for being there. She looked at me and said, "You'll continue to be blessed." I thought, 'She's just saying that because she's a nun.' But she was right. As time passes, I continue to be blessed for being on the reservation.

CHAPTER THIRTY-FOUR

A HAPPY ENDING

Before I left for the reservation, Grey Wolf gave me a stone to take with me. He told me it would give me strength and with strength comes comfort. I kept that stone in my desk drawer at school and I would take it out every so often and hold it in my hand. Grey Wolf told me I could give it away, but I could never sell it. When I came back to California, I gave it to Andrew, my former student at Santa Maria de las Rosas who always sent me the most encouraging emails. It always made me laugh when he would write about how cold it was in Los Angeles as I was walking to and from school in negative-degree temperatures. He had been loyal to me the whole time I was away, so the stone that Grey Wolf had given me at the beginning of my journey I passed along to Andrew.

And now for you the reader, when you get to the point in life where it gets a little too difficult and you don't think you can go on, just say to yourself, "If she can survive a Montana winter, I can get through this." And you'll do just fine.

END NOTES

[1] Page 106
The Red Ribbon movement began in Calexico, California in reaction to the murder of DEA Agent "Kiki" Camarena in 1985 in Mexico. His neighbors and friends wore red ribbons to honor their fallen hero and the sentiment spread and soon red ribbons became the symbol of alcohol, tobacco, and drug abuse and violence prevention. In 1988 Red Ribbon Week became a national event organized by the National Family Partnership chaired by then First Lady Nancy Reagan. (*redribbon.org)

[2] Page 110
After being forced to relocate south to the Southern Cheyenne Reservation in what is now present-day Oklahoma, a band of Northern Cheyenne fled north to escape the horrible conditions they were forced to endure, primarily lack of food and inadequate health care. Led by Chief Dull Knife and Little Wolf, the flight became known as The Northern Cheyenne Exodus. After reaching Nebraska, the group decided to separate. Chief Dull Knife's division followed him to Red Cloud Agency where the Lakota were, while the rest followed Little Wolf and returned to the Powder River territory.

During a blinding storm, Chief Dull Knife's people fell into the hands of the U.S. military. Forced to surrender they were confined to Fort Robinson in northwestern Nebraska. The Northern Cheyenne stayed at Fort Robinson for the next few months while their future remained uncertain. The U.S. military wanted Chief Dull Knife and his people to return south, while Chief Dull Knife wanted his people to return to the Pine Ridge Reservation. On January 3, the U.S. military took drastic measures to pressure Chief Dull Knife to return south. (Boyle, Alan p.251- 297 Holding Stone Hands: On the Trail of the Cheyenne Exodus, University of Nebraska Press(1999) ISBN 0-8032-1294-1

Fort Robinson was barricaded, the heat was cut off and the Indians were not given food or water for four days. (Berthrong, Donald p.3-17 The Cheyenne and Arapaho Ordeal: Reservation and Agency Life in the Indian Territory, 1875-1907 Norman: University of Oklahoma Press 1992 ISBN 987-0-8061-2416-2)

The breakout proved to be a disaster for the Northern Cheyenne. Only a few had successfully escaped, including Chief Dull Knife, while many more were wounded and captured. (Monnett, John H., p.149 — 156, Tell Them We Are Going Home: The Odyssey of the Northern Cheyennes, University of Oklahoma Press 2001, ISBN 0-8061-3303-1)

By 1884, the Northern Cheyenne were able to return to the Tongue River Reservation. (Berthrong, Donald p. 26 - 47 The Cheyenne and Arapaho Ordeal: Reservation and Agency Life in the Indian Territory, 1875-1907 Norman: University of Oklahoma Press 1992 ISBN 987-0-8061-2416-2

[3] Page 126
Kateri, also known as Lilly of the Mohawks, was born in what is today Auriesville, New York to the Algonquin-Mohawk tribe. She became a convert to Catholicism at the age of nineteen, living only another five years. However her short life of chastity and virtue became a shining example for Natives and Catholics alike. Pierre Cholenec, S.J. (1696). The Life of Catherine Tekakwitha, First Iroquois Virgin. Archived from the original on July 25, 2011. Retrieved 2012-02-18. She was beatified in 1980 and canonized by Pope Benedict XVI in 2012. Pope Canonizes 7 Saints, Including 2 With New York Ties, The New York Times, 22 October 2012.

[4] Page 161
Guy de Galard, Native Life, Western Life & Style: Cowboys and Indians French wine expert took his beads and dreams to American Indians 2009.

ALSO BY LUELLA WAGNER

The Seven Directions of the Medicine Wheel:
A practical guide for everyday living based on Native American teachings

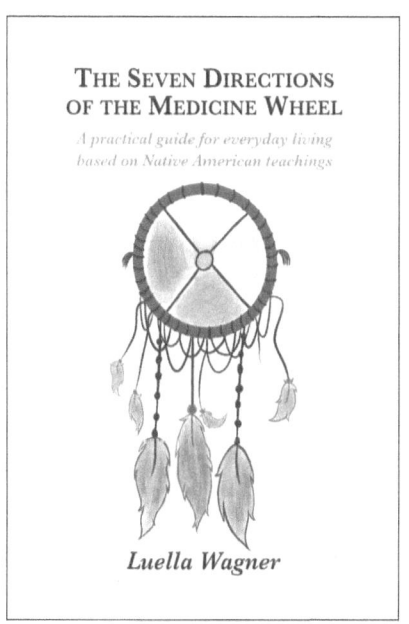

The Seven Directions of the Medicine Wheel will bring balance, harmony, and beauty into your life by working with the Creator and applying simple and practical lessons found in nature. Based on Native American teachings, the book focuses on one's spiritual, emotional, physical, and mental health through all the stages of life. Ideal book for students, educators, administrators, and business executives.

Available through Amazon.com and www.luellawagner.com

www.ingramcontent.com/pod-product-compliance
Lightning Source LLC
Chambersburg PA
CBHW030550080526
44585CB00012B/327